Beneath the Surface: Principles for Navigating Economic Cycles

Edward J. Allen

Published by Revvity, Inc, 2025.

BENEATH THE SURFACE: PRINCIPLES FOR NAVIGATING ECONOMIC CYCLES

First edition. August 7, 2025.

Written by Edward J. Allen.

Table of Contents

INTRODUCTION

UNDERSTANDING THE MACHINE

In the complex, ever-shifting world of finance and economics, patterns often masquerade as chaos. Markets swing, currencies falter, economies rise and fall, and geopolitical tensions ripple through asset prices. To the untrained eye, it can feel random. But beneath the surface, there is structure. There is a rhythm. There is a machine at work.

This book is about understanding that machine.

At its core, an economy is not a mystery. It's a system a relatively simple one, in fact driven by the behavior of individuals, businesses, and governments making millions of decisions each day. These decisions form transactions. Transactions form markets. Markets form economies. And when we zoom out far enough, patterns emerge. Cycles repeat. Consequences follow causes.

The ability to recognize these patterns to understand how economic and financial systems truly function is one of the most powerful tools any investor, policymaker, or global citizen can possess. It offers clarity in uncertainty, discipline in volatility, and foresight in an age defined by information overload.

Why This Book?

Over the past century, we've witnessed extraordinary economic events: the Great Depression, the Bretton Woods era, stagflation in the 1970s, Japan's lost decade, the dot-com bubble, the 2008 global financial crisis, and the COVID-19 pandemic. Each of these episodes seemed different at the time, but they were governed by the same underlying principles reactions within the economic machine.

This book is designed to demystify those principles. It brings together timeless economic truths, practical investment wisdom, and historical case studies to help readers build a deep and durable understanding of how economies and markets work. It is a synthesis of systems thinking, data-driven frameworks, and actionable strategy.

Whether you are a new investor trying to make sense of macroeconomic news, a policymaker tasked with making high-stakes decisions, or a curious observer seeking a more informed worldview, the pages that follow will provide clarity.

The Structure of This Book

The book is divided into five parts, each building on the last:

- **Part I: The Economic Machine in Motion** introduces the conceptual framework what economies are, how they operate through credit and productivity, and the role human behavior plays in shaping outcomes. We explore both short-term and long-term debt cycles, as well as what drives sustainable productivity growth.
- **Part II: Principles for Investment Decision-Making** offers insight into how economic cycles affect asset prices and provides a strategic lens for making intelligent, long-term investment decisions.
- **Part III: Geopolitics, Policy & Macro Risks** dives into the global forces shaping the future of economics and investing from shifting world orders to currency dynamics and fiscal tensions.
- **Part IV: Building a Resilient Investment Framework** focuses on how to develop robust, emotionally disciplined strategies that can withstand crisis and uncertainty.
- **Part V: Looking Ahead – The Future of Investing** explores the tectonic shifts underway in technology, sustainability, and global cooperationequipping readers to think generationally.

Each chapter includes historical parallels, data-driven analysis, and frameworks you can apply directly to your investment thinking or policy perspective.

A Word on Perspective

Much of the thinking in this book draws inspiration from systems-based approaches to economics, notably the frameworks pioneered by Ray Dalio, as well as insights from decades of macroeconomic study, investing practice, and geopolitical analysis. But this is not a one-theory-fits-all narrative. It's a guide to thinking independent thinking in a world where conventional wisdom often fails.

You won't find predictions here. You'll find principles. And principles, unlike predictions, can help you navigate uncertainty with greater confidence and clarity.

So whether the next chapter in the global economy brings inflation or deflation, growth or stagnation, peace or conflict this book is here to help you make sense of it. And most importantly, to prepare.

Let's begin.

CHAPTER 1
ECONOMIES AS MACHINES

1.1 The Economy as a Machine: A Systems View

At first glance, an economy can appear overwhelmingly complex. There are millions of variables at play interest rates, prices, wages, trade balances, taxes, spending patterns, asset valuations, and countless others. But when stripped down to its fundamental components, the economy functions like a machine a large, dynamic system composed of relatively simple parts interacting in repeatable ways.

Just like an engine runs on fuel and transfers energy to motion, an economy runs on **transactions** the basic unit of economic activity. A transaction occurs whenever a buyer exchanges money or credit for goods, services, or assets. Every transaction reflects a decision someone deciding that what they receive is more valuable than what they give. Multiply that decision-making process by billions, and you have an economy in motion.

But this machine is not made of metal or circuits. It is a **cybernetic system** a feedback-driven, adaptive network where information, behavior, and incentives continuously shape outcomes. Inputs (like monetary policy, technological innovation, or consumer preferences) flow through economic agents (households, firms, governments), generating outputs (production, employment, inflation), which in turn feed back into the system through price signals, wage adjustments, and policy responses.

This makes economies **complex adaptive systems** not entirely predictable, but not random either. Patterns emerge over time due to repeated interactions, which is why history often echoes in financial cycles. The economic machine, then, is not static but **evolves**, shaped by innovation, policy, demography, and, most crucially, human behavior.

Within this machine, there are **three fundamental driving forces**:

1. **Productivity growth**
2. **The short-term debt cycle (business cycle)**

3. **The long-term debt cycle (deleveraging and restructuring)**

These three forces move at different speeds. Productivity advances slowly and steadily, like the pistons of an engine. Short-term debt cycles move faster, driven by changes in credit, interest rates, and sentiment. Long-term cycles unfold over decades, reflecting deep structural imbalances that require painful corrections.

Understanding these three forces is key to interpreting most economic phenomena booms, busts, recoveries, and stagnations without getting lost in the noise of daily data or media narratives.

1.2 Transactions: The Building Blocks of Economies

Every economic activity whether it's a person buying groceries, a business investing in new equipment, or a government issuing bonds can be boiled down to a transaction. **Transactions are the atoms of the economic universe**, and all economic flows national income, trade balances, inflation, GDP are merely large aggregates of trillions of these individual exchanges.

Every transaction involves three key components:

- **A buyer**
- **A seller**
- **A medium of exchange** (money or credit)

While money is straightforward cash or digital currency exchanged for goods or services **credit is more nuanced and powerful.** Credit is essentially **a promise to pay later**, and it introduces time into the transaction. It enables buyers to obtain goods or services now, in exchange for future income. Credit transforms present capacity and reshapes future obligations.

Historically, economies grew more robust and interconnected as credit markets matured. With credit, economic activity no longer needed to wait for income to be earned. Businesses could borrow to invest in machinery or hire workers. Consumers could purchase homes, cars, and appliances without saving for years. Governments could finance infrastructure, defense, or welfare programs by issuing bonds.

But this convenience comes at a cost: **debt**. Credit becomes debt the moment it is issued, and that debt becomes a claim on future income. The more debt accumulates, the more vulnerable the economy becomes to changes in interest rates, asset prices, or income levels.

The Digital Shift in Transactions

In recent decades, the **nature of transactions has evolved dramatically**. The rise of digital platforms, mobile banking, and block chain-based currencies has transformed how people exchange value. Platforms like PayPal, Apple Pay, and Alipay allow billions of transactions to occur daily without cash. Crypto-Currencies, though still volatile and controversial, offer a decentralized way to transact outside of traditional financial systems.

Moreover, the rise of **fin-tech** (financial technology) has created new layers of credit creation and transaction facilitation. Peer-to-peer lending platforms, algorithmic underwriting, and buy-now-pay-later (BNPL) services have made credit more accessible but also more opaque and potentially unstable.

This evolution has accelerated transaction velocity the speed at which money changes hands which, in turn, impacts how quickly economic shocks can spread and how rapidly policy changes take effect. In essence, **the engine of the economy now spins faster**, requiring more precise monitoring and control.

Credit: The Amplifier

When credit expands, spending rises, businesses hire more workers, and output grows. But when credit contracts because of rising interest rates, tighter lending standards, or falling consumer confidence spending falls, businesses cut back, and economies slow down or enter recession.

This cyclical nature of credit means that **transactions are not just neutral events**; they are shaped by, and in turn shape, the broader economic cycle. That's why understanding the behavior of borrowers and lenders what motivates them, how they assess risk, and how they respond to incentives is essential for grasping economic dynamics.

In short, while **productivity** is the only long-term source of sustainable economic growth, **credit cycles** create the **short- and medium-term fluctuations** that define business cycles, asset bubbles, and financial crises. Transactions are the levers that move the economy forward or pull it back.

1.3 Productivity: The True Engine of Growth

While credit and consumption can accelerate economic activity, they do not, by themselves, create wealth. **Only productivity doing more with less creates real, lasting wealth**. It is the invisible hand that lifts living standards, improves national income, and sustains economic progress over generations.

What is Productivity?

At its core, **productivity** refers to how efficiently resources labor, capital, and technology are used to produce goods and services. It's typically measured in two ways:

- **Labor productivity**: Output per hour worked or per worker. This is the most commonly referenced measure in economic discussions.
- **Total Factor Productivity (TFP)**: A broader measure that captures output relative to the combined input of both labor and capital. TFP attempts to quantify the effects of innovation, improved management, and technological advancement.

An increase in productivity means that the same number of workers, or the same level of investment, produces more output. Over time, this increase translates into **higher incomes, more leisure time, and improved quality of life**.

Sources of Productivity Growth

Productivity gains can come from many sources, including:

- **Technological innovation**: New tools, machines, and software that streamline or automate tasks.
- **Education and skills**: A better-educated and more skilled workforce can perform tasks more efficiently and adapt to new methods.
- **Capital investment**: More or better equipment and infrastructure can raise output per worker.
- **Organizational efficiency**: Improvements in management, logistics, and systems (e.g., lean manufacturing or agile workflows) reduce waste and increase output.
- **Scale and specialization**: As firms grow and specialize, they often become more efficient through economies of scale.

Not all productivity improvements are dramatic. Many are small and incremental slight changes to how a task is done or subtle innovations in process. But thanks to **compounding over time**, even modest improvements can have profound long-term effects.

The Quiet Driver of Wealth

Productivity doesn't grab headlines like stock market crashes or inflation scares. It advances quietly, often beneath the radar of daily news cycles. But make no mistake: **it is the most important determinant of long-term prosperity**.

Consider the difference between two economies growing at different productivity rates. An economy with 1% annual productivity growth will double its output in about 70 years. But if productivity grows at 3% annually, that same doubling occurs in just 24 years. That's the power of compounding improvements.

The Productivity Paradox

Despite rapid advances in technology, some economists have observed what's known as the **productivity paradox**: a puzzling slowdown in measured productivity growth, especially in developed economies, despite the digital revolution.

Possible explanations include:

- **Lag effects**: It takes time for new technologies to diffuse and reshape economic structures.
- **Measurement gaps**: Productivity statistics may not fully capture intangible gains from services, software, or data.
- **Sectoral shifts**: As economies mature, more activity shifts toward slower-growing service sectors.

Understanding and resolving this paradox is crucial for future policy and investment decisions.

Productivity vs. Consumption

It's tempting to equate economic health with consumption more spending, higher GDP, bustling markets. But consumption without productivity is **unsustainable**. It can be fueled by debt, but eventually, that debt must be repaid. True economic progress must come from **producing more real value**, not just moving money around faster.

That's why central banks and policymakers, while managing short-term cycles, must ultimately focus on the **foundations of productivity** education, infrastructure, innovation, and institutional quality. These are the levers that drive the economy forward in the long run.

In sum, **credit and transactions create the rhythm**, but **productivity sets the melody**. A society that prioritizes efficiency, innovation, and learning plants the seeds of enduring prosperity.

1.4 Credit: The Double-Edged Sword

Credit is one of the most powerful tools in the economic machine. Used wisely, it can drive innovation, job creation, and growth. Used recklessly, it can destabilize entire economies. It is both a **multiplier of prosperity** and a **mechanism of collapse** which is why understanding how credit functions is vital to navigating economic cycles.

The Power of Credit

At its best, credit transforms **potential** into **reality**. A business borrows money to expand its operations, build a new factory, or hire skilled workers.

That activity creates jobs, generates income, and boosts productivity. Likewise, a family that takes out a mortgage can buy a home, stimulating construction, home goods sales, and financial services.

This is the **credit multiplier effect**: a single loan can set off a chain reaction of economic activity. For example:

1. A small business borrows $100,000 to expand.
2. It hires more staff, increasing household incomes.
3. Those households then spend more, boosting demand elsewhere in the economy.
4. The increased demand encourages further investment, and the cycle continues.

Credit Becomes Debt

But credit isn't free it creates **debt**, and that debt must eventually be repaid. The moment a loan is issued, a future obligation is born. If income grows in line with debt, repayment is manageable. But when **debt grows faster than income**, the system becomes fragile.

This fragility often hides behind rising asset prices and economic optimism. Borrowers assume tomorrow will be better than today. Lenders, seeing past success, extend more credit. This can create a **credit bubble**, where asset prices rise not because of underlying value, but because of speculative borrowing.

Eventually, the bubble bursts.

A Case in Point: The 2008 Global Financial Crisis

Perhaps the most vivid example of credit turning dangerous is the **2008 global financial crisis**. In the years leading up to the crisis:

- Credit expanded rapidly in the housing market.
- Financial institutions packaged mortgage debt into complex securities (mortgage-backed securities, CDOs).
- Lenders relaxed standards, offering mortgages to borrowers with little or no income verification (subprime loans).
- Housing prices soared, and optimism ran high.

But this boom was unsustainable. When borrowers began to default, the value of these securities collapsed. Banks faced massive losses, trust in the system evaporated, and credit froze. The result: the worst economic downturn since the Great Depression.

This event was not an anomaly it was a **classic case of the credit cycle in action.**

Modern Credit Instruments and Risks

Credit has become more complex in the 21st century. Beyond traditional loans, modern economies now rely on:

- **Derivatives**: Financial contracts whose value is derived from underlying assets.
- **Shadow banking**: Non-bank financial institutions that engage in credit creation with less regulation.
- **Private equity leverage**: Firms taking on large amounts of debt to buy, restructure, or flip businesses.
- **Consumer credit innovations**: Services like buy-now-pay-later, which blur the lines between consumption and borrowing.

These tools increase efficiency but also **amplify systemic risk**. Because credit is often intertwined with leverage and speculation, the effects of mispricing risk can cascade rapidly through global markets.

The Cycle of Credit Expansion and Contraction

The economy's dependence on credit creates **inherent cycles**:

- During **expansions**, credit is easy, optimism grows, and borrowing increases.
- At some point, debt levels exceed the ability to repay, leading to **defaults.**
- Fear replaces greed. Credit tightens, spending slows, and the economy **contracts.**
- Eventually, debts are reduced or restructured, confidence returns, and **the cycle restarts.**

These cycles don't signal a malfunction of the machine they **are the machine**. They are how the economy self-corrects, albeit often painfully.

Credit and Inequality

One often-overlooked consequence of credit expansion is its impact on **inequality**. Asset owners tend to benefit more from credit booms, as they can leverage rising asset prices. Wage earners, by contrast, often bear the brunt of contractions. This dynamic has widened wealth gaps in many advanced economies, leading to social and political strain.

Summary

Credit is essential to a dynamic economy it accelerates investment, facilitates innovation, and allows for intertemporal consumption. But it must be managed carefully. Excessive borrowing, particularly for non-productive purposes (like speculative real estate or consumer goods), leads to instability. Understanding the role and risks of credit is key to managing the ups and downs of the economic machine.

1.5 Human Behavior: The Invisible Driver

While the economic machine may sound mechanical and rational, at its core, it is powered by **human beings** imperfect, emotional, and influenced by perception as much as reality. Behind every transaction, investment, policy, and purchase is a human decision shaped by beliefs, biases, and behavioral patterns.

The Rational and the Irrational

Classical economics assumes that people are **rational actors** they make decisions to maximize utility based on available information. But real-world behavior often deviates from this model. In fact, modern research in **behavioral economics** shows that people are predictably irrational. They:

- Follow the crowd (herding behavior)
- Overestimate recent trends (recency bias)
- Ignore unlikely but devastating risks (normalcy bias)
- Avoid losses more intensely than they seek gains (loss aversion)

These biases don't just affect individual decisions—they **shape entire economies.**

Feedback Loops and Sentiment

Economic cycles are amplified by human emotions. In good times, people become optimistic. They take more risks, borrow more, and invest heavily. This inflates asset prices, which reinforces their optimism a **positive feedback loop.**

Conversely, when the economy slows or markets fall, fear spreads. People cut back on spending, pull out investments, and hoard cash. This drives further contraction a **negative feedback loop.**

Examples:

- The **dot-com bubble** of the late 1990s: Investors believed internet companies could only go up, pouring money into unprofitable startups.
- The **2008 housing crash**: Buyers assumed home prices would rise forever, leading to reckless lending and speculation.
- The **COVID-19 market panic**: A sudden loss of confidence triggered a global sell-off, despite central bank assurances.

Each of these episodes demonstrates how **psychology magnifies economic swings** turning modest corrections into full-blown crises or recoveries into exuberant booms.

"Animal Spirits"

Economist John Maynard Keynes introduced the concept of **"animal spirits"** to describe how instincts and emotions drive economic decisions. Confidence, optimism, fear, and panic are not merely background noise they **move markets and shape policies.**

For instance:

- A consumer confident in their job prospects is more likely to take a loan or spend on durable goods.
- An entrepreneur who believes in the future may start a business despite uncertain forecasts.
- A central bank may adjust policy not only based on data but also to manage **expectations** and **narratives.**

In this sense, **expectations become self-fulfilling.** When enough people believe the economy will grow, they act accordingly and growth happens.

Narrative Economics

Recent work by economist Robert Shiller explores **"narrative economics"** how stories, not just data, shape economic behavior. Popular narratives (e.g., "real estate always goes up," "tech stocks are the future," "inflation is dead") spread through society and influence investment, consumption, and policy.

These narratives, like viruses, can become contagious. They may be based in fact or fiction, but once accepted, they **guide mass behavior** and become real in their consequences.

Policymaking and Behavioral Insight

Because behavior drives volatility, central banks and governments increasingly act as **managers of confidence**, not just controllers of money. This is why:

- Central bank communications (forward guidance) are carefully worded to signal intentions.
- Political leaders make optimistic statements even during downturns to

calm markets.
- Emergency fiscal measures are announced with emphasis on speed and scale to restore belief in recovery.

Ultimately, managing an economy is as much about **shaping expectations** as it is about manipulating interest rates or budgets.

The Human Variable

Economies are not just mathematical models they are **social systems**. Every chart or index represents human decisions. This means that economic outcomes are never purely deterministic. They are subject to swings in emotion, social mood, and collective belief.

Recognizing the role of human behavior in economic cycles doesn't make them avoidable but it does make them understandable. It reminds us that economic policy is not just about numbers; it's about **narratives, trust, and psychology**.

1.6 Feedback Loops: Income ↔ Spending ↔ Production

One of the most important dynamics in any economy is the **feedback loop** between income, spending, and production. This loop is deceptively simple, yet it forms the **core mechanism** by which economic growth (or contraction) unfolds.

Let's revisit this loop in more depth:

1. **Spending drives production:**
   When consumers, businesses, or governments spend money, it increases demand for goods and services. In response, companies ramp up production to meet that demand.
2. **Production generates income:**
   To increase output, businesses need labor, equipment, and services. They hire more workers, pay wages, purchase supplies, and invest in capital. All of these activities **distribute income** to households and other firms.
3. **Income leads to more spending:**
   As households and firms earn more, they have more to spend. That spending restarts the cycle ideally at a higher level, fueling a **self-reinforcing expansion**.

This dynamic forms a **positive feedback loop**, where growth in one area amplifies growth in others. The key is **momentum**. As long as spending increases faster than costs, the loop builds upon itself.

The Amplifier: Credit

This loop becomes far more powerful when **credit** enters the system. With credit, people and businesses can spend **more than they currently earn**, accelerating the loop beyond what income alone would support.

For example:

- A household takes out a loan to buy a car.
- The car dealer earns revenue and pays employees.
- Those employees spend at grocery stores and restaurants.
- The original borrowed money ends up **cascading** through multiple layers of the economy.

This is why credit is so tightly linked to the **velocity of money** the speed at which money moves through the system.

The Downward Spiral: Negative Feedback Loops

However, feedback loops don't only work in one direction. In a downturn, the same loop works in reverse:

- Spending slows.
- Businesses reduce production and cut jobs.
- Incomes fall.
- Consumers and firms reduce spending further.

This **negative feedback loop** can trigger a recession, especially when it becomes self-reinforcing. What begins as a drop in demand can escalate into a widespread economic slowdown if not counteracted.

The Role of Marginal Propensity to Consume (MPC)

A key concept in understanding these loops is the **marginal propensity to consume (MPC)** how much of each additional dollar of income people are likely to spend.

- **Low-income households** often have a high MPC they spend most of what they earn.
- **Wealthier households** tend to save more, which slows the loop unless their savings are recycled into investments or redistributed through fiscal policy.

This is why fiscal stimulus that targets lower-income groups can be more effective in reviving an economy. A dollar sent to someone likely to spend it **generates more immediate economic activity** than one sent to someone likely to save it.

Fiscal Policy: Directly Modulating the Loop

Governments can intervene in these loops through **fiscal policy** spending and taxation. In recessions, governments often increase spending or cut taxes to inject money directly into the loop.

For example:

- Stimulus checks increase household spending.
- Infrastructure projects hire workers and purchase materials.
- Tax cuts leave more money in consumers' pockets.

These measures **jump-start the loop**, ideally triggering private-sector production and income generation that sustains the cycle once public support is reduced.

Conversely, during booms, governments may run surpluses, reduce spending, or increase taxes to avoid overheating the economy and inflating asset bubbles.

A System in Constant Oscillation

The income-spending-production loop is a perpetual **oscillator** it rarely moves in a straight line. Small shocks can tip the balance one way or the other, and external factors (interest rates, energy prices, wars, pandemics) can amplify or suppress its momentum.

Recognizing this loop allows policymakers, investors, and households to anticipate shifts. It also reinforces a key truth: **economies are not linear systems.** They are feedback-driven, nonlinear, and sometimes volatile especially when external shocks collide with internal imbalances.

1.7 The Role of Central Banks in Managing the Machine

Given the volatility inherent in credit-fueled feedback loops and behavior-driven cycles, modern economies require a stabilizing force **this is the role of central banks.** Like skilled mechanics tuning a complex engine, central banks monitor and adjust the economy's performance to maintain balance between growth, inflation, employment, and financial stability.

What Do Central Banks Do?

At a fundamental level, central banks manage the **cost and availability of money and credit.** Their core tools include:

- **Setting interest rates**: The primary instrument to control borrowing and spending.
- **Open market operations**: Buying or selling government securities to influence liquidity.
- **Reserve requirements**: Controlling how much banks must hold versus lend.
- **Forward guidance**: Shaping expectations by signaling future policy directions.
- **Quantitative easing (QE)**: Injecting liquidity into the financial

system by purchasing long-term assets, especially during crises.

These tools aim to **smooth the business cycle**, preventing overheating during booms and softening downturns during recessions.

How Interest Rates Work

Interest rates act like a **brake or accelerator** on economic activity:

- When central banks **lower rates**, borrowing becomes cheaper. Businesses invest, consumers spend, and economic activity increases.
- When they **raise rates**, borrowing becomes more expensive. This cools demand, curbs inflation, and slows the economy.

The goal is to maintain **price stability and full employment** without letting inflation run too high or growth stall.

Central Banks as Confidence Managers

Beyond monetary tools, central banks also play a psychological role. In moments of panic or uncertainty, **confidence collapses faster than cash flow**. The mere act of a central bank committing to stability can calm markets.

For example:

- In March 2020, when the COVID-19 crisis sent markets into freefall, the U.S. Federal Reserve launched massive emergency lending facilities, slashed interest rates to near zero, and initiated a $700 billion QE program. The announcements alone helped stabilize confidence, even before the full effects took hold.

This illustrates the growing importance of **central bank communication**. Often, markets react more to expectations and tone than to actual policy moves.

Quantitative Easing: A Modern Tool

Quantitative easing, first widely used during the 2008 financial crisis, represents a shift from traditional monetary policy. Instead of targeting short-term rates alone, central banks **buy longer-term assets** (like government bonds or mortgage-backed securities) to inject liquidity into the financial system and lower long-term borrowing costs.

QE is especially useful when interest rates are already near zero a situation known as the **zero lower bound**, where traditional tools lose effectiveness. However, QE comes with potential side effects:

- **Asset price inflation**: It can push up prices of stocks, bonds, and real estate.
- **Wealth inequality**: Asset owners benefit more than wage earners.
- **Moral hazard**: Markets may expect central banks to rescue them from every downturn.

The Liquidity Trap and Limits of Monetary Policy

Sometimes, despite low interest rates and ample liquidity, people or businesses **don't want to borrow or spend** this is known as a **liquidity trap**. It's a scenario where monetary policy loses traction because confidence is low or debt levels are already too high.

In these cases, monetary policy needs to be paired with **fiscal policy** government spending and taxation to generate demand directly.

This reveals a key limitation: **central banks cannot create real productivity**. They can influence short-term demand, but not long-term innovation, infrastructure, or education. These are in the domain of governments, institutions, and private enterprise.

Central Banks in Developed vs. Emerging Economies

Central banking plays out differently across the world:

- In **developed economies**, central banks tend to operate independently, with well-developed financial systems and strong policy credibility.
- In **emerging markets**, central banks often face political pressure, weaker institutions, or volatile capital flows. They may be forced to defend their currency, control inflation amid unstable demand, or manage debt in foreign currencies.

This makes their job more complicated and often riskier, especially in times of global turbulence.

Central Banks and the Future

Looking ahead, central banks are being called to address **new challenges**:

- **Climate change**: Should they factor environmental risks into lending and investment criteria?
- **Digital currencies**: Central bank digital currencies (CBDCs) could reshape monetary policy, payments, and financial inclusion.
- **Inequality**: Some argue central banks should consider distributional effects of their policies.
- **Financial stability**: As financial markets evolve with fin-tech and crypto, central banks must adapt regulation and oversight.

In a world of growing complexity, central banks remain essential but they are not omnipotent. They can guide, stabilize, and incentivize but not transform the fundamentals of an economy.

1.8 Case Study: The U.S. Economy Post-World War II

The period following World War II offers a vivid, real-world demonstration of the economic machine in motion an intricate interplay of transactions, feedback loops, credit expansion, productivity growth, human behavior, and policy intervention on an enormous scale. The transformation of the U.S. economy from wartime austerity to postwar prosperity illustrates how economies rebuild, reinvent, and respond to changing dynamics.

Demobilization and Rebuilding (1945–1950)

After the Allied victory in 1945, the United States faced a daunting challenge: demobilize its massive wartime economy and reintegrate millions of returning soldiers into civilian life without falling into depression. Many economists and policymakers feared a repeat of the Great Depression, expecting a collapse in demand as war production ceased.

Instead, the opposite happened. The U.S. entered a powerful expansionary phase driven by **pent-up consumer demand, government support, and productive capacity**.

Key drivers included:

- **The GI Bill**: Offered veterans access to higher education, home loans, and business support, creating a generation of skilled workers and homeowners.

- **Pent-up savings**: Wartime rationing and limited consumer options had led to high personal savings, which were unleashed in the form of spending.
- **Industrial reconversion**: Factories shifted from military hardware to consumer goods cars, appliances, housing materials meeting soaring demand.

This period saw a powerful **positive feedback loop**:

- Government programs injected income into households.
- Consumer spending surged.
- Businesses ramped up production and hiring.
- Rising employment further boosted income and spending.

The Suburban Boom and Credit Expansion (1950s–1960s)

The 1950s and 60s witnessed the emergence of **middle-class America**, defined by homeownership, automobile culture, and consumer abundance. At the heart of this transformation was the **expansion of credit**.

Key developments:

- **Mortgages and suburbanization**: The Federal Housing Administration (FHA) backed affordable long-term loans. Suburban developments like Levittown became symbols of mass housing.
- **Consumer credit**: Credit cards and installment plans became widespread, enabling Americans to buy now and pay later cars, televisions, refrigerators, and more.
- **Government spending**: Massive investments in highways (Interstate Highway Act, 1956), defense, and research (NASA, DARPA) stimulated both demand and innovation.

This era demonstrated the economic engine at full throttle:

- **Productivity was rising** thanks to automation, improved logistics, and scale.
- **Credit was fueling demand**, amplifying the production-spending-

income loop.

- **Confidence was high**, supported by rising wages, stable inflation, and growing household wealth.

Productivity and Innovation

This postwar boom was not just driven by credit it was underpinned by genuine **productivity gains**:

- **Technological innovation**: Wartime R&D spilled into civilian industries jet engines, radar, synthetic materials, and eventually computers.
- **Workforce education**: The GI Bill produced millions of college-educated workers, raising skill levels across industries.
- **Infrastructure investment**: Roads, ports, power grids, and schools expanded national productive capacity.

These factors created a virtuous cycle **productivity gains increased income, which supported demand without generating excessive inflation**. This helped sustain growth through much of the 1950s and 60s.

Global Positioning and the Dollar's Role

Another powerful dynamic was America's **unique global economic position**. Postwar, the U.S. was the only major industrial economy left intact. It became the **engine of global trade** and the **issuer of the world's reserve currency** under the Bretton Woods system.

This meant:

- U.S. exports boomed as Europe and Asia rebuilt.
- The dollar became the anchor for global trade and finance.
- America could run deficits and fund them with dollar-denominated debt, exporting its credit system abroad.

This global demand for dollars also allowed the U.S. to support expansive domestic programs without immediate inflationary consequences though this would change later.

Cautionary Notes: The Seeds of Future Instability

While the postwar period is remembered as an economic golden age, it also **planted seeds of long-term imbalance**:

- **Rising consumer debt**: Households became increasingly reliant on credit.
- **Government commitments ballooned**: Social Security, Medicare, defense spending, and entitlements began growing faster than revenues.
- **Dollar dominance created imbalances**: As U.S. imports rose, foreign central banks accumulated U.S. assets, distorting global capital flows.
- **Inflationary pressures emerged**: By the late 1960s, government spending on the Vietnam War and Great Society programs, combined with loose monetary policy, began to overheat the economy.

These imbalances would later manifest in the **stagflation** of the 1970s a rare and painful combination of rising prices and stagnant growth.

Lessons from the Postwar Boom

The U.S. post-WWII experience illustrates the economic machine in motion at scale:

- **Productivity growth** provided a strong, sustainable base for rising living standards.
- **Credit expansion**, when matched by rising income and confidence, amplified growth.
- **Government policy** both fiscal and monetary was crucial in guiding the transition and maintaining stability.
- **Human behavior** confidence, optimism, risk-taking fueled innovation and expansion.

But it also reveals the risks of overextension. Even golden ages contain vulnerabilities, and every boom carries within it the conditions for the next correction.

CHAPTER 2

THE SHORT-TERM DEBT CYCLE

2.1 Understanding the Short-Term Debt Cycle

The short-term debt cycle also known as the **business cycle** is one of the most well-studied phenomena in economics. It describes the rhythmic rise and fall in economic activity that typically plays out over 5 to 10 years. These cycles involve periods of expansion, peak, contraction (recession), and recovery.

At the core of these movements lies one crucial dynamic: **credit expansion and contraction.**

Credit, when easily available, fuels spending and investment beyond what current incomes alone can support. But this artificial boost is temporary. As debt service obligations mount, spending slows, credit tightens, and the economy contracts. Then the cycle begins again.

Unlike long-term debt cycles, which may take decades to unfold, short-term debt cycles are frequent and observable in everyday economic and market behavior.

2.2 Anatomy of a Short-Term Debt Cycle

To understand how this cycle operates, we can break it down into four main phases:

1. Expansion (Credit Growth Phase)

- Interest rates are low
- Credit is cheap and accessible
- Businesses invest; consumers borrow to spend
- Asset prices (stocks, real estate) rise
- Employment and incomes grow

This is the **boom phase**, characterized by optimism, rising leverage, and strong economic performance.

2. Peak

- Capacity constraints emerge (e.g., labor or raw material shortages)

- Inflationary pressures build
- Central banks begin to tighten policy to prevent overheating
- Borrowing starts to slow

The system reaches a **tipping point**, often unnoticed until it's too late.

3. Contraction (Recession Phase)

- Interest rates rise, making debt more expensive
- Consumers and businesses cut back
- Asset prices fall as expectations adjust
- Defaults increase; credit tightens further
- Layoffs occur, reducing incomes and spending

This is the **downturn**, often marked by falling GDP and declining confidence.

4. Recovery

- Inflation subsides
- Central banks cut interest rates
- Credit slowly resumes
- Pent-up demand and policy stimulus begin to lift economic activity

The economy begins to recover, setting the stage for a new cycle.

2.3 Credit and Money: The Inflation–Deflation Tug-of-War

The short-term debt cycle creates a constant balancing act between **inflation and deflation**.

- When too much money chases too few goods, prices rise inflation.
- When credit contracts and spending falls, prices drop deflation.

Central banks must navigate this trade-off carefully. Their tools aim to avoid both **runaway inflation** and **deflationary spirals**, both of which can be deeply destabilizing.

The **Federal Reserve**, for example, targets a 2% inflation rate, considered healthy for economic stability. Too little inflation is seen as dangerous because it can lead to wage stagnation and lower investment. Too much inflation erodes purchasing power and can destabilize savings and business plans

2.4 Central Bank Tools and the Fight for Stability

Central banks play a pivotal role in managing the short-term debt cycle. Their toolkit includes:

1. Interest Rate Policy

By raising or lowering the **federal funds rate**, the central bank influences the cost of borrowing. This affects everything from mortgages to corporate loans.

- Lower rates → encourage borrowing → stimulate spending
- Higher rates → discourage borrowing → slow the economy

2. Open Market Operations

Central banks buy or sell government securities to influence liquidity in the banking system. Buying securities injects cash; selling them removes cash.

3. Reserve Requirements

By adjusting the amount of reserves banks must hold, central banks can influence how much money banks can lend.

4. Forward Guidance

Central banks communicate their future policy intentions to influence market expectations. Confidence is a powerful tool, and forward guidance helps shape behavior before actual policy shifts.

5. Quantitative Easing (QE)

QE involves buying longer-term securities (often government bonds) to inject liquidity into the financial system. This tool became central after the 2008 crisis and again during the COVID-19 pandemic.

These tools are meant to manage economic momentum. But they are not perfect. Policy lags, unpredictable human behavior, and external shocks often limit effectiveness.

2.5 Case Study: Federal Reserve Responses Since 2008

The 2008 financial crisis was a defining moment for modern central banking and a vivid illustration of the short-term debt cycle in action.

The Boom Before the Bust

Before 2008, low interest rates and lax credit standards fueled a massive housing boom. Borrowers with poor credit "subprime" borrowers were able to secure mortgages, often with adjustable-rate terms that hid the true cost of debt.

- Home prices soared
- Consumers felt wealthy and borrowed more
- Banks securitized mortgages and passed on risk to investors
- Risk models failed to capture the systemic fragility

This was a textbook example of **credit-driven expansion** coupled with overconfidence and risk blindness.

The Crisis Unfolds

When housing prices began to fall and adjustable-rate mortgages reset, defaults surged. This exposed the fragile underpinnings of the credit boom:

- Mortgage-backed securities collapsed in value
- Banks faced liquidity crises and stopped lending
- The financial system seized up
- A full-scale credit contraction triggered the Great Recession

In this environment, central banks had to act decisively.

The Fed's Response

- **Interest rates** were slashed to near zero
- **QE programs** were launched, injecting trillions into financial markets
- **Forward guidance** assured markets that policy would remain accommodative
- New lending facilities were created to support banks and businesses

These actions stopped the downward spiral, stabilized the financial system, and laid the groundwork for recovery. But they also created side effects:

- Asset prices (stocks, housing) rebounded rapidly exacerbating inequality
- Corporate debt rose to new highs
- Long-term dependence on low interest rates was baked into the system

Post-COVID Echoes

The pandemic in 2020 triggered similar central bank actions only on a larger and faster scale. Lessons from 2008 were applied aggressively: rates were cut instantly, trillions were injected into markets, and government stimulus packages supported household incomes directly.

Again, a sharp contraction was followed by a robust, stimulus-fueled recovery until inflation pressures returned in 2022–2023, prompting a new tightening cycle.

2.6 The Side Effects of Credit-Driven Growth

While credit expansion can drive growth in the short run, it often comes with long-term trade-offs. The post-2008 and post-COVID periods offer clear examples of both the benefits and the dangers of heavy reliance on credit and monetary stimulus.

Asset Inflation and Inequality

When central banks lower interest rates or implement quantitative easing, they primarily stimulate demand through **asset markets**. Investors respond by buying equities, real estate, and bonds, which drives prices up.

While this can boost **wealth effects** (people spend more when they feel wealthier), the gains are not evenly distributed:

- **Asset holders** (typically wealthier individuals) benefit disproportionately.
- **Wage earners** and those without financial assets see fewer benefits.

This divergence contributes to rising **wealth inequality**, a growing political and economic challenge in many advanced economies.

Distorted Risk-Taking

Prolonged periods of low interest rates can also **encourage excessive risk-taking**:

- Investors chase yield in riskier assets.
- Companies borrow heavily to buy back shares or expand aggressively.
- "Zombie firms" (unprofitable businesses sustained by cheap credit) survive longer than they should.

These distortions can make the financial system more fragile and prone to future crises.

Debt Dependency

Each time the system is stabilized by credit, more debt is added to the economy. Eventually, this leads to a situation where:

- **Interest payments** consume a large portion of income.
- **New borrowing** becomes less effective at stimulating growth.
- The economy becomes more sensitive to rate hikes.

This is why repeated short-term cycles if not paired with real productivity growth can erode long-term resilience.

2.7 The Limits of Monetary Policy

Central banks have powerful tools, but they are not omnipotent. Over time, the effectiveness of monetary policy **diminishes** if it is overused or used in isolation from fiscal policy and structural reforms.

Liquidity Trap and Diminishing Returns

When interest rates are already near zero, further cuts have limited impact. This is known as the **liquidity trap**, where:

- People prefer to hold cash rather than invest.
- Banks may not lend, even with low rates.
- Consumers may not borrow, especially if they are already in debt or uncertain about the future.

Quantitative easing and asset purchases can support markets, but they may not trickle down effectively into real economic activity.

Misallocation of Capital

Easy money environments can lead to poor investment decisions. Capital flows into speculative assets instead of productive investments like innovation, infrastructure, or education. This **misallocation** undermines long-term growth.

Loss of Credibility and Inflation Risks

If central banks maintain ultra-loose policy for too long, they risk losing credibility. Expectations of persistent inflation or the fear that central banks will be unable to tighten policy can lead to **runaway inflation**, currency depreciation, or capital flight.

We saw early signs of this in 2021–2022, when inflation returned more sharply than central banks anticipated, forcing a rapid and painful reversal of easy-money policies.

2.8 Lessons from the Short-Term Debt Cycle

Looking across decades of data and dozens of countries, several consistent lessons emerge about short-term debt cycles:

1. **They are inevitable.** Human behavior, especially regarding credit and confidence, ensures that economic expansions will always be followed by contractions.
2. **Credit is a powerful amplifier.** It speeds up both booms and busts. When managed well, it supports investment and growth. When mismanaged, it leads to crisis.
3. **Central banks can stabilize but not solve structural problems.** Their tools are best suited to managing short-term fluctuations, not long-term economic health.
4. **Early interventions are cheaper than late responses.** Delayed tightening in an overheating economy, or slow support in a downturn, worsens the cycle.
5. **Long-term growth depends on productivity, not credit.** Relying solely on debt-fueled expansion is a short-sighted strategy.

2.9 Summary: A Cycle Worth Mastering

The short-term debt cycle is not a flaw in the system it is the system. The rise and fall of credit, the ebb and flow of interest rates, the rhythms of confidence and caution these are as fundamental to economics as gravity is to physics.

To navigate this cycle as an investor, policymaker, or business leader requires both:

- **Macro awareness**: Recognizing where the economy is in the cycle, and how central banks are likely to respond.
- **Strategic discipline**: Avoiding overexposure during booms and positioning intelligently for recoveries.

CHAPTER 3

THE LONG-TERM DEBT CYCLE

3.1 What Is the Long-Term Debt Cycle?

The long-term debt cycle plays out over a span of **50 to 75 years** and culminates in profound economic shifts—debt crises, deflationary deleveraging, structural resets, and new monetary regimes. Unlike the short-term debt cycle, which is repetitive and relatively predictable, the long-term debt cycle is rare, severe, and system-altering.

At its core, the long-term cycle is about the **accumulation of debt over generations**, fueled by:

- Persistent use of credit to drive economic activity
- Political reluctance to tolerate recessions or austerity
- Monetary policies that prioritize short-term growth over long-term sustainability

Over time, debt grows **faster than income**, until the burden becomes unsustainable. At this point, economies must undergo a painful process of **deleveraging**, during which debt levels are reduced through defaults, inflation, restructuring, or some combination thereof.

3.2 The Lifecycle of a Long-Term Debt Super-cycle

The long-term debt cycle typically unfolds in **four major phases**:

1. The Foundation (Low Debt, Productive Growth)

- A period of low debt-to-income ratios
- Credit is used productively for innovation, infrastructure, education
- Economic growth is strong and sustainable
- Central banks and governments maintain fiscal and monetary discipline

This phase often follows a major economic reset like a war or previous debt crisis.

2. The Accumulation Phase (Rising Leverage)

- Credit becomes more widely available and cheaper
- Households, businesses, and governments borrow more
- Asset prices rise, encouraging further borrowing
- Consumption increases faster than productivity

During this phase, debt grows **faster than income**, but the system appears stable because interest rates are low and asset values are rising.

3. The Tipping Point (Debt Saturation)

- Debt service costs begin to crowd out spending
- Borrowers struggle to meet obligations
- Economic growth slows, despite more borrowing
- Central banks may lower rates to zero or near-zero

At this stage, **monetary policy loses effectiveness**. More debt creates diminishing returns. Structural imbalances build beneath the surface.

4. Deleveraging (Crisis and Reset)

- A credit crunch or asset crash triggers defaults
- Debt is reduced through bankruptcies, austerity, inflation, or restructuring
- Governments intervene with fiscal stimulus and monetary expansion
- New financial frameworks emerge (e.g., new currencies, debt mutualization)

This phase can take a decade or more. It typically results in a **reallocation of wealth**, a **new monetary order**, and often a shift in **geopolitical power**.

3.3 Historical Examples of Long-Term Debt Cycles

Understanding the long-term debt cycle requires looking at real-world examples. Three stand out as instructive:

The Great Depression and the 1929 Crash (U.S.)

The Build-Up:

- The 1920s were marked by rapid credit expansion and speculative investment
- Consumer goods (e.g., cars, radios) were often bought on installment plans
- Stock market speculation was rampant often with borrowed money

The Collapse:

- In 1929, the bubble burst, and the stock market crashed
- Banks failed in waves; credit contracted sharply
- The economy entered a deflationary spiral

The Deleveraging:

- Wages and prices fell
- The U.S. abandoned the gold standard in 1933 to reflate the economy
- Public works and social safety nets were introduced (e.g., New Deal)

Outcome:

- The Great Depression reshaped capitalism, birthed modern central banking, and led to WWII

Japan's Lost Decade (1990s–Present)
The Build-Up:

- In the 1980s, Japan experienced an enormous asset bubble fueled by easy credit and speculation
- Land and stock prices soared, far outpacing fundamentals

The Collapse:

- In 1991, the bubble burst real estate and equity prices crashed
- Banks were left with bad debts; lending dried up

The Deleveraging:

- Japan entered a prolonged period of stagnation
- Interest rates fell to zero; QE and fiscal stimulus were used repeatedly
- Debt-to-GDP soared, but growth remained sluggish

Outcome:

- Japan avoided crisis-level unemployment or social unrest but sacrificed growth
- Its experience is now viewed as a textbook case of **"balance sheet recession"**

The Global Debt Super-cycle (2008–Present)
The Build-Up:

- Over several decades, developed economies used credit to finance growth
- Global debt (public and private) ballooned to over 350% of GDP
- Asset bubbles and wealth inequality rose dramatically

The Collapse:

- The 2008 financial crisis exposed the fragility of the system
- Massive bailouts and unprecedented monetary easing followed

The Deleveraging:

- Rather than allowing broad defaults, policymakers opted to "kick the can"
- QE became permanent; interest rates stayed ultra-low
- Global debt has continued rising, shifting increasingly to sovereign balance sheets

Outcome:

- Many believe we are still in the late stages of a long-term debt cycle
- Warning signs of structural fragility persist (high debt, weak growth, populism)

3.4 Warning Signs of a Long-Term Debt Crisis

To prepare for a potential long-term debt correction, it's essential to recognize early warning signs:

- **Debt-to-GDP ratios rising unsustainably**
- **Interest payments crowding out government spending**
- **Monetary policy at or near zero-bound with no room to maneuver**
- **Asset valuations disconnected from fundamentals**
- **Productivity stagnation despite high investment**
- **Rising populism and political polarization**
- **Loss of confidence in currency or central bank independence**

These indicators suggest that the system is stretched and a **restructuring event** is likely within the horizon.

3.5 Navigating a Deleveraging Environment

Deleveraging the process of reducing debt in an economy is inherently painful. Unlike recessions caused by short-term demand shocks, deleveraging often requires **long-term behavioral, fiscal, and structural adjustments**.

There are four primary ways a society can reduce its overall debt burden:

1. Austerity (Spending Less)

- Governments and households cut spending to repay debt.
- GDP declines; unemployment typically rises.
- This can deepen a recession if applied too aggressively.

2. Debt Defaults and Restructuring

- Debtors fail to pay or renegotiate terms.
- Lenders absorb losses; credit is impaired.
- While painful, this "clears the slate" and allows growth to resume.

3. Wealth Redistribution

- Higher taxes, social transfers, or asset seizures are used to reduce inequality or public debt.
- Politically volatile, often leading to social unrest or populist movements.

4. Printing Money (Monetary Inflation)

- Central banks create money to buy debt or finance deficits.

- If used carefully, this can reduce real debt burdens without immediate crisis.
- If used excessively, it risks **currency debasement and hyperinflation**.

In practice, **most deleveraging use a combination** of these strategies. The challenge is finding a balance that reduces debt burdens **without sparking political collapse or runaway inflation**.

3.6 Tools for Investors in Long-Term Deleveraging Cycles

Investing during a deleveraging period requires a very different approach than in expansionary cycles. Here are key strategies and tools:

1. Prioritize Capital Preservation

- Focus on **high-quality, low-volatility assets** (e.g., U.S. Treasuries, gold, select cash-rich equities).
- Consider inflation-linked bonds (TIPS) during monetary inflation episodes.

2. Diversify Across Environments

- Use **diversification across geographies, asset classes, and currencies** to mitigate systemic risk.
- The "All Weather" or **risk parity** strategy is particularly effective in uncertain regimes.

3. Monitor Policy and Political Risk

- Fiscal and monetary policy becomes dominant market drivers.
- Track central bank balance sheets, deficit spending, and shifts in political leadership.

4. Be Opportunistic During Forced Deleveraging

- Asset prices often overshoot on the downside.
- Crises can create **once-in-a-generation opportunities** if you are liquid and disciplined.

5. Stay Agile

- Long-term debt cycles are unpredictable in timing and scope.
- Avoid rigid strategies; adopt **rules-based, scenario-tested frameworks**.

3.7 Structural Reform: The Long-Term Solution

While monetary policy can buy time and fiscal stimulus can soften blows, **only structural reforms can resolve the underlying issues** of a long-term debt cycle.

Key reforms may include:

- **Rebalancing consumption and investment** toward productive sectors
- **Improving education, innovation, and labor mobility**
- **Fixing broken tax systems and entitlement programs**
- **Reforming financial regulations** to curb speculative excess
- **Encouraging entrepreneurship and capital formation**

These reforms are difficult, politically sensitive, and slow to deliver results but they are the **only path to sustainable recovery** once debt burdens have outgrown the system's ability to support them.

3.8 Long-Term Debt Cycles and Shifts in Global Power

Long-term debt cycles often coincide with, or contribute to, **major geopolitical transformations**. As one empire or economic system declines under the weight of debt and dysfunction, others rise to fill the vacuum.

Historical examples include:

- The fall of the British Empire post-WWI, giving rise to U.S. dominance.
- The collapse of the Soviet Union under fiscal and ideological strain.
- The current global shift toward a **multipolar world**, with **China**, **India**, and **sovereign wealth-heavy nations** asserting more influence.

Long-term debt cycles, in this sense, are more than financial they are **civilization turning points.**

3.9 Summary: Preparing for the Inevitable Reset

Long-term debt cycles don't unfold often, but when they do, they reshape the economic and political landscape for generations.

Key takeaways:

- **They are driven by decades of credit accumulation**, supported by short-term cycles that mask the growing imbalance.
- When debt levels become unsustainable, **deleveraging is unavoidable.**
- There is no painless path out only a choice between different trade-offs.

- **Investors must think defensively**, maintain liquidity, and be prepared for sudden regime shifts.
- **Policymakers must prioritize structural reform** over short-term stimulus.

In the next chapter, we will focus on the **true driver of long-term prosperity productivity growth** and how innovation, education, and infrastructure determine whether a nation thrives or stagnates after a debt reset.

CHAPTER 4

PRODUCTIVITY GROWTH AND ECONOMIC DEVELOPMENT

4.1 Productivity: The True Engine of Economic Progress

Economic growth can come from several sources credit expansion, fiscal stimulus, resource exploitation but only one source is **sustainable over time**: **productivity growth**.

Productivity refers to the amount of output generated per unit of input most commonly, labor. When workers can produce more goods or services in the same amount of time, the economy becomes more efficient. This leads to:

- Higher real incomes
- Lower costs of production
- Better standards of living
- Greater competitiveness on the global stage

While debt can temporarily boost spending, and asset bubbles can create short-term wealth effects, **only productivity improvements generate enduring wealth**.

4.2 The Drivers of Productivity Growth

1. Technological Innovation

Advancements in technology tools, machines, software, and automation allow workers and businesses to produce more with less.

- The printing press, the steam engine, the internet, and now artificial intelligence (AI) have transformed economies.
- Innovation drives both **process efficiency** (doing things better) and **product innovation** (creating new things).

2. Human Capital Development

A skilled, educated, and healthy workforce is essential for productivity.

- **Education systems** equip workers with technical and cognitive skills.
- **Healthcare systems** ensure a longer and more productive life span.

- **On-the-job training** helps employees adapt to changing technologies and markets.

Human capital investments have **compound effects** each generation benefits from the advancements of the previous one.

3. Infrastructure

Reliable infrastructure lowers the cost of doing business and improves efficiency across sectors.

- **Physical infrastructure**: roads, railways, ports, and utilities
- **Digital infrastructure**: broadband, cloud platforms, cyber-security
- **Institutional infrastructure**: stable legal systems, property rights, contract enforcement

Nations with modern, efficient infrastructure enjoy lower transaction costs and faster productivity gains.

4. Capital Formation

Investment in physical capital factories, tools, machinery allows labor to become more productive. However, it must be **intelligent investment** aligned with real demand and efficient processes.

5. Research and Development (R&D)

R&D spending leads to breakthroughs that shift entire industries. Government and private sector R&D must be coordinated for optimal outcomes.

4.3 Capital Formation vs. Human Capital

Economic development requires both **physical capital** and **human capital** but the balance between the two varies by stage of development.

In Early Development:

- Building factories, roads, power grids takes priority.
- Capital-intensive investment delivers faster growth.

In Advanced Economies:

- Gains from capital investment diminish over time.
- Improving **human capital and innovation systems** becomes essential.

For example:

- South Korea's rise in the late 20th century relied on heavy capital investment in manufacturing and education.
- Germany combines capital efficiency with a world-class vocational training system.
- The U.S. has sustained long-term growth through universities, entrepreneurship, and technological leadership.

The synergy between educated workers and modern tools is the sweet spot for productivity.

4.4 Policy Prescriptions for Long-Term Growth

Governments that wish to foster sustained economic growth must take a strategic approach across several dimensions:

1. Education and Training

- Invest in early childhood education, literacy, STEM fields
- Expand access to vocational and technical education
- Adapt to future-of-work demands (coding, data, AI, soft skills)

2. Infrastructure Investment

- Maintain and modernize physical infrastructure
- Support digital connectivity in rural and underserved areas
- Encourage public-private partnerships in large-scale projects

3. R&D and Innovation Ecosystems

- Provide incentives for private-sector R&D
- Fund research institutions and universities
- Create hubs for collaboration (e.g., Silicon Valley model)

4. Regulatory Efficiency

- Streamline business registration and licensing
- Protect intellectual property while promoting competition
- Reduce corruption and bureaucratic friction

5. Open Trade and Investment

- Facilitate global integration where beneficial
- Attract foreign direct investment with transparent rules
- Avoid protectionism that stifles innovation

4.5 Comparative Case Study: U.S. vs. China vs. Europe

United States: Innovation and Entrepreneurial Ecosystem

- Strengths: world-class universities, venture capital, start-up culture
- Weaknesses: declining education quality in parts of the country, aging infrastructure
- Long-term outlook: remains competitive but vulnerable to underinvestment in human capital and rising inequality

China: State-Directed Capitalism and Infrastructure Boom

- Strengths: rapid capital formation, efficient infrastructure roll-out, massive investments in AI and manufacturing
- Weaknesses: demographic decline, debt overhang, political centralization limiting innovation
- Long-term outlook: strong potential, but depends on rebalancing from capital to consumption and services

Europe: Quality of Life and Institutional Strength

- Strengths: social cohesion, high-quality public goods, advanced manufacturing
- Weaknesses: slower innovation cycles, rigid labor markets, demographic pressures
- Long-term outlook: stable but less dynamic unless structural reforms are embraced

Each region demonstrates a different model of economic development. The most successful nations will be those that can combine **flexibility, investment, and inclusiveness.**

4.6 The Role of the Private Sector in Development

While governments provide the foundation, private enterprise is the **engine of innovation and productivity**.

- Startups drive disruption in old industries.
- Corporations scale new technologies globally.
- Competitive markets encourage continuous improvement.

To maximize impact, the private sector needs:

- Access to capital
- Stable legal frameworks
- Efficient labor markets
- Fair competition and reduced monopolistic behavior

Public-private collaboration, when managed transparently, often yields better outcomes than either sector operating alone.

4.7 Summary: Productivity Is Destiny

Debt cycles may define the rhythm of economies, but productivity defines their **trajectory**.

Key takeaways:

- **Productivity growth is the only sustainable source of real economic improvement**.
- It depends on a combination of human capital, capital investment, infrastructure, and innovation.
- Government policy must shift from short-term stimulus to long-term planning.
- Nations that invest in productivity become wealthier and more resilient over generations.

CHAPTER 5

INVESTING IN THE CONTEXT OF ECONOMIC CYCLES

5.1 Why Economic Context Matters in Investing

Every investment decision is made within a specific economic context. Markets don't exist in a vacuum they are heavily influenced by cycles in:

- Credit availability
- Inflation and interest rates
- Economic growth and contraction
- Monetary and fiscal policy

Investors who ignore these cycles often find themselves **fighting the tide** buying risky assets at the top, or panicking during bottoms. Conversely, those who understand macroeconomic dynamics can position portfolios **proactively** rather than **reactively**.

The central premise of this chapter is simple:

Your investment strategy should adapt to where the economy is in the cycle.

This requires more than watching headlines it demands a framework that combines economic analysis, asset class sensitivity, and psychological discipline.

5.2 The Interplay Between Economic Phases and Asset Performance

Each phase of the economic cycle favors different types of assets. Here's a simplified breakdown:

1. Early Expansion

- Credit is cheap, growth is recovering
- Central banks are accommodative
- Inflation is low or just starting to rise

Winning Assets:

- Equities (especially cyclicals)
- High-yield bonds

- Commodities (early-stage rebound)

2. Late Expansion

- Growth is strong but peaking
- Inflation begins to rise
- Central banks may tighten policy

Winning Assets:

- Equities (especially value, industrials)
- Real estate
- Inflation-protected securities (TIPS)

3. Contraction / Recession

- Growth slows or contracts
- Corporate earnings fall
- Credit tightens

Winning Assets:

- High-quality government bonds
- Defensive stocks (consumer staples, utilities)
- Gold (as a hedge)

4. Recovery / Early Cycle

- Central banks lower rates
- Fiscal stimulus often introduced
- Risk appetite returns cautiously

Winning Assets:

- Equities (growth stocks, tech)
- Credit (investment-grade and high-yield)
- Real assets (REITs, infrastructure)

Understanding this interplay allows investors to **tilt portfolios tactically** without attempting to time markets perfectly.

5.3 Tactical vs. Strategic Investing

Strategic Investing

- Long-term asset allocation based on goals, risk tolerance, and time horizon
- Minimal changes regardless of economic cycle
- Designed to weather all environments

Tactical Investing

- Short-to-medium term adjustments based on macro conditions
- Requires more active management and research
- Can improve returns or reduce risk when executed well

Key Insight:

Tactical investing should complement not replace strategic allocation. It adds flexibility but must be governed by **clear rules and risk management.**

5.4 Timing the Market vs. Preparing for Change

Attempting to predict exact tops and bottoms in the market is extremely difficult, even for professionals. The goal should not be **timing**, but rather **readiness**.

Strategies for Preparedness:

- Maintain diversified exposure across asset classes
- Use **leading indicators** (e.g., yield curves, PMIs, credit spreads) to assess risks
- Set rebalancing rules to automatically adjust exposure
- Keep **dry powder** (cash or near-cash instruments) for opportunistic deployment

5.5 The Bubble Detector Checklist

One of the most powerful tools for avoiding catastrophic losses is learning to recognize **bubbles**. Ray Dalio, among others, has developed frameworks to assess whether an asset or market is in a bubble.

Here's a distilled version of a **Bubble Detector Checklist**:

1. **Prices are high relative to traditional measures.**
2. **Prices are discounting unrealistic future expectations.**
3. **New buyers are entering the market at increasing rates.**
4. **Borrowing is fueling purchases (high leverage).**
5. **Buyers believe prices will never fall.**
6. **Assets are being bought for speculative gains, not intrinsic value.**
7. **Narratives are replacing fundamentals.**

If most of these boxes are checked, caution is warranted. Even if the bubble continues temporarily, the **risk/reward ratio becomes unfavorable**.

5.6 Macro Frameworks for Investment Decisions

To apply economic insights systematically, investors can use structured macro frameworks. These often include:

- **Economic phase maps** (growth vs. inflation quadrants)
- **Regime-based modeling** (e.g., stagflation, reflation, deflation)
- **Monetary policy tracking** (hawkish/dovish cycles)
- **Cross-asset correlations and stress testing**

Using these tools, investors can:

- Build portfolios suited to each environment
- Prepare contingency plans for downside scenarios
- Avoid anchoring biases by focusing on data

5.7 Case Illustration: Investing Through the 2008–2020 Cycle

This real-world example illustrates cycle-aware investing:

- **2008–2009:** Safe haven assets outperformed (Treasuries, gold). Stocks crashed.
- **2010–2012:** Recovery trade (equities, commodities) thrived with QE support.
- **2013–2019:** Slow but stable expansion growth stocks, tech led the way.

- **2020 COVID Crash:** Quick deflation followed by unprecedented stimulus. Agile investors rotated into tech, then cyclicals.
- **2021–2023:** Inflation re-emerged; central banks pivoted. Commodities, value stocks, and energy outperformed briefly.

Each of these stages favored different assets cycle-informed investors had a roadmap.

5.8 Summary: The Cycle Is the Strategy

Investment success isn't just about choosing good assets it's about understanding when they are good. Economic cycles shape the performance of every asset class.

Key takeaways:

- Markets are cyclical. Your portfolio should be too.
- Asset performance varies by economic phase prepare accordingly.
- Use macro frameworks, not emotions, to make investment decisions.
- Avoid the temptation of perfect timing—aim instead for **contextual alignment**.

CHAPTER 6

THE IMPORTANCE OF DIVERSIFICATION

6.1 Why Diversification Matters

In an uncertain, cyclical, and often irrational world, diversification is one of the few strategies that consistently improves **risk-adjusted returns.**

At its core, diversification means:

Not putting all your eggs in one basket and ensuring your baskets aren't all tied together.

The logic is simple:

- No one can consistently predict which asset, sector, or region will outperform.
- Correlations between assets change over time.
- Surprises both positive and negative are inevitable.

Diversification smoothes the ride it doesn't eliminate risk, but it **protects against large draw downs** and ensures participation in up trends across different environments.

6.2 The "Holy Grail" of Investing: Uncorrelated Bets

Ray Dalio famously described diversification as the **"Holy Grail of Investing."** According to Dalio, if an investor can build a portfolio of high-quality, **uncorrelated return streams**, they can dramatically reduce risk without sacrificing return.

How It Works:

- Imagine you have 15 to 20 investments.
- Each has a **positive expected return**, but low or negative correlation with the others.
- When some assets struggle, others perform well.
- The portfolio's volatility decreases, and draw downs are shallower.

Key Insight:

With enough uncorrelated assets, the total portfolio risk falls **exponentially**, even if each asset is risky on its own.

This is how sophisticated hedge funds and institutional investors achieve **consistent performance without relying on forecasts.**

6.3 Common Misconceptions About Diversification

Despite its simplicity, diversification is often misunderstood. Here are some prevalent myths:

◈ ***"I own 30 stocks—I'm diversified."***

If those stocks all move together in a market downturn, you're not diversified. **Sector and style exposure matter.**

◈ ***"Diversification lowers returns."***

Diversification may **lower potential maximum gains**, but it **improves consistency** which often leads to better **compounded long-term returns**.

◈ ***"Gold and stocks are always uncorrelated."***

Correlations **change over time**. Assets that were uncorrelated can move together in crises. Rely on **data**, not assumptions.

6.4 Building a Diversified Portfolio: Practical Strategies

True diversification requires **exposure to different return drivers**, not just different assets.

1. Diversify Across Asset Classes

- **Equities** (U.S., international, emerging markets)
- **Fixed Income** (government, corporate, high-yield, inflation-linked)
- **Real Assets** (real estate, commodities, infrastructure)
- **Cash and Short-Term Instruments**

2. Diversify by Geography

- Economies operate on different cycles.
- Currency movements can also create diversification benefits.

3. Diversify by Strategy

- **Growth vs. Value**
- **Momentum vs. Mean Reversion**
- **Active vs. Passive**

4. Use Alternatives Thoughtfully

- Hedge funds, private equity, and managed futures can provide **uncorrelated alpha** if carefully selected.

6.5 Risk Parity and Balanced Portfolios

Risk parity is an advanced diversification strategy that allocates based on **volatility contribution** rather than capital weighting.

Traditional Portfolio:

- 60% stocks / 40% bonds
- Heavily dependent on equity returns

Risk Parity Portfolio:

- Allocates more capital to low-volatility assets (like bonds)
- Balances risk across asset classes
- Often uses leverage to equalize return contribution

Benefits:

- Greater resilience in recessions and inflation shocks
- Smoothed return profile
- Outperforms traditional allocations in multi-regime environments

6.6 Dalio's "All Weather Portfolio"

Ray Dalio's **All Weather Portfolio** is a famous example of risk-balanced investing. It's designed to perform reasonably well across all four economic regimes:

Economic Environment	Winning Asset Classes
Rising Growth + Low Inflation	Stocks, corporate bonds
Falling Growth + Low Inflation	Government bonds
Rising Inflation + Falling Growth	Commodities, gold
Rising Growth + Rising Inflation	Stocks, commodities

A typical All Weather Portfolio might look like:

- 30% U.S. stocks
- 40% long-term bonds
- 15% intermediate-term bonds
- 7.5% gold
- 7.5% commodities

While this isn't optimized for maximum gain, it's optimized for **balance**, helping protect against **blind spots and bias.**

6.7 Behavioral Benefits of Diversification

Diversification is not only mathematical it's **psychological.**

- It prevents overconfidence in any one thesis.
- It softens emotional reactions to volatility.
- It makes it easier to stay invested through turbulence.

Investing is as much about staying in the game as it is about finding the best returns.

Diversification gives you the confidence to endure the journey.

6.8 Summary: The Only Free Lunch in Finance

Economies are uncertain. Markets are volatile. Predictions are often wrong. Diversification is the only strategy that:

- Protects against the unknown
- Reduces risk without sacrificing expected return

- Enhances emotional resilience and long-term consistency

CHAPTER 7

DESIGNING INVESTMENT SYSTEMS

7.1 Why Investment Systems Matter

Most investors underperform not because they lack intelligence or access to information, but because they fall victim to **emotions, biases, and inconsistencies**. They buy high out of euphoria, sell low out of fear, and shift strategies in reaction to recent outcomes.

A well-designed investment system solves this by providing:

- **Structure**: Clear rules for action
- **Consistency**: Discipline across time and market regimes
- **Clarity**: Reduced ambiguity and decision paralysis

"The key is to develop a system that takes the emotion out of investing and replaces it with logic, data, and repeatable processes."

The world's best hedge funds including Bridgewater, AQR, Renaissance Technologies, and others operate on **rules-based systems** that automate investment decisions based on macro, fundamental, and quantitative inputs.

7.2 The Core Elements of a Good Investment System

To design an effective system, it must address several critical components:

1. Investment Philosophy

- Are you trend-following or mean-reverting?
- Are you seeking growth, income, or capital preservation?
- What is your time horizon and drawdown tolerance?

This is the **foundation** of your system your beliefs about how markets work.

2. Signal Generation

- What indicators or data trigger buy/sell decisions?
- Examples: momentum signals, valuation thresholds, economic data

3. Position Sizing

- How much capital do you allocate per trade or asset?
- Use volatility, conviction, or risk budgets to guide this.

4. Risk Management

- How do you limit losses? (e.g., stop-losses, volatility controls)
- How do you ensure no single asset dominates portfolio risk?

5. Execution

- How will you implement your trades? (automated, manual, DCA, etc.)
- Consider costs, slippage, and liquidity constraints.

6. Review and Adaptation

- When and how do you evaluate system performance?
- What metrics (Sharpe ratio, drawdown, win/loss %) do you track?

A robust system is not static it evolves based on **evidence**, not emotion

7.3 Back testing: Learning from the Past

Back testing involves applying your system to **historical data** to evaluate how it would have performed.

Key Guidelines for Effective Back testing:

- Use **long timeframes** and multiple market regimes.
- Avoid **over fitting** a model that performs perfectly in the past may fail in the future.
- Include **transaction costs, slippage, and taxes** for realism.
- Track **draw downs** and not just total returns.

Back testing won't guarantee future performance, but it will **reveal weaknesses and stress points** before real money is at stake.

7.4 Stress Testing: Preparing for Extremes

Stress testing evaluates how your system performs during **extreme events** market crashes, rate spikes, geopolitical shocks.

Scenarios to Test:

- 2008 financial crisis
- COVID-19 crash (2020)
- 1970s stagflation
- Dot-com bubble burst (2000–2002)
- Sudden rate hikes (e.g., 2022 tightening cycle)

Ask:

- Does the system blow up?
- Does it preserve capital?
- Does it adapt or sit idle?

Good systems should **survive first and thrive second.**

7.5 Removing Emotion from Investment Decisions

Emotional investing is the enemy of compounding. A systematic approach removes:

- **Fear and greed cycles**
- **Performance chasing**
- **Panic selling in downturns**
- **Overconfidence during rallies**

Methods to Reinforce Discipline:

- Automate rebalancing and trade execution
- Use checklists before making discretionary overrides
- Maintain an investment journal to log decisions and reasoning

Radical Transparency and Feedback

Inspired by Bridgewater's culture, some investors adopt **radical transparency** openly reviewing past decisions and challenging assumptions.

This feedback loop is essential for refining systems and avoiding stagnation.

7.6 From Discretionary to Systematic: A Practical Transition

For many investors, the shift to a systematic approach is gradual.

Start with:

- Clear asset allocation rules

- Scheduled rebalancing (e.g., quarterly)
- Risk limits (e.g., max drawdown thresholds)

Then expand to:

- Data-driven asset rotation models
- Automated trade triggers
- Full portfolio simulators

Even partial systematization can yield major benefits in consistency and peace of mind.

7.7 The Future: AI and Algorithmic Investing

Machine learning and AI are increasingly shaping modern investment systems.

- **Natural language processing** scans news for market signals
- **Sentiment analysis** tracks public mood
- **Quantitative models** adapt in real time to new data

These tools are powerful but also complex and risk-prone. Use them to **augment human judgment**, not replace it blindly.

7.8 Summary: Build the Machine Before You Enter the Market

Markets are noisy. Emotions are volatile. But systems provide stability.
Key takeaways:

- Systems-based investing reduces emotional error.
- A good system is clear, adaptable, and risk-aware.
- Back testing and stress testing validate your model before real-world application.
- Discipline, feedback, and continuous improvement are the path to mastery.

With a strong system in place and diversification as a core principle, we now move into **Part III**, where we examine the **geopolitical and macro risks** that threaten or reinforce these investment foundations.

CHAPTER 8

THE CHANGING WORLD ORDER

8.1 From Unipolarity to Fragmentation: A New Global Landscape

The post–World War II era largely represented U.S.-led unipolarity, characterized by liberal trade, open markets, and multilateral institutions. That era is ending. We are moving into an era of **multipolar competition**, economic blocs, and geopolitical risk as a persistent and structuring force in markets.

This shift is redefining how nations interact transforming globalization into **geo-economics**, where states deploy economic tools tariffs, capital controls, investment policies for strategic advantage.

8.2 The Rise of Multipolar Power Centers

Today, global influence is increasingly shared among multiple centers, not dominated by a single hegemon:

- **China**, via its Belt & Road Initiative, Global Security and Civilization Initiatives, is expanding economic and ideological influence globally.
- **The Global South** encompassing Asia, Africa, Latin America is taking on diplomatic and economic leadership roles, forming new alliances and asserting influence in forums like BRICS, and demanding more representation in institutions like the IMF and UN.
- **Europe and India** are forging regional blocs and pursuing strategic autonomy, balancing Western and Eastern spheres of influence.
- This new structure is less hierarchical and more networked, with power distributed across regional and ideological lines.

8.3 Competing Orders and Strategic Rivalries

As new power centers emerge, competing visions of international norms are intensifying:

- China emphasizes **sovereignty, non-intervention, and state-led development**, positioning itself as an alternative model to Western liberalism.
- The U.S. and its allies are reinforcing democratic norms, market

liberalism, and integrated security systems through platforms like NATO, PGII (the G7's Global Infrastructure Initiative), and coordination on supply chain resilience. This ideological competition is reshaping trade rules, ESG standards, and investment flows. Europe, for example, has begun integrating **defense and energy security** into ESG frameworks areas that traditionally fell outside such considerations.

8.4 The Axis of Upheaval: A Shadow Bloc Emerges

A strategic coalition of anti-Western autocracies China, Russia, Iran, North Korea is increasingly coordinating military, technological, and diplomatic efforts. Analysts term this alignment the "Axis of Upheaval."This bloc is challenging Western-led norms through alternative institutions, joint operations, and narrative control creating a **dual-track international system**.

8.5 Financial Fragmentation and Currency Realignment

Geopolitical conflict is reshaping global financial architecture:

- Nations are **de-risking reliance** on traditional U.S.-led systems like SWIFT, increasingly adopting China's CIPS network and cross-border CBDCs.
- The strength of the U.S. dollar is contested, as regions build **regional currency blocs** Europe developing a "Global Euro," and Asia bolstering the yuan.

This fragmentation means **asset and currency diversification** is no longer optional it's essential for managing geopolitical risk.

8.6 Historical Cycles: Empire, Debt, Leadership

Economic and geopolitical shifts follow recurring patterns. Ray Dalio's "Big Cycle" framework highlights how rising powers challenge declining ones often through debt-fueled expansion.

The **Kindleberger Trap** warns that global stability depends not only on who is rising, but who fills the leadership void. If no one publicly provides global goods (like currency stability or security), disorder follows.

We may be entering such a trap if the U.S. retreats without viable institutions stepping in, global cooperation and order could unravel.

8.7 Investing Amid New Power Structures

What do these shifts mean for investors?

- **Diversify globally**: Exposure limited to U.S. equities is increasingly riskier international and regional assets are gaining traction.
- **Prepare for shocks**: Geopolitical events like sanctions, trade wars, or conflicts now move markets fundamentally. Refresh risk frameworks accordingly.
- **Access new corridors**: Emerging hubs such as China, India, Southeast Asia offer growth potential but require scrutiny of political, legal, and operational risks.
- **Re-evaluate currency and asset correlations**: Global regimes are diverging. Gold, real assets, foreign equity and bond exposure may act differently than in past cycles.

8.8 Summary: Navigating the New World Order

The former global consensus open markets, shared values, and U.S.-led institutions is fragmenting. We now live in a world where:

- Power is **distributed among multiple poles.**
- Economic policy is both **market-driven and strategically directed.**
- Financial and governance systems are **regionalizing and diversifying.**
- Risks are **geopolitical as much as macroeconomic.**

For investors, success in this environment requires infrastructure diversification, macro risk frameworks, geopolitical awareness, and strategic agility.

CHAPTER 9

MONETARY SYSTEMS AND CURRENCY DYNAMICS

9.1 The Foundation of Monetary Systems

At the heart of every economic system lies a monetary framework: **how money is created, managed, and trusted.** Whether gold-backed or fiat, the design of a monetary system determines the credibility of a nation's currency, its trade balances, its inflation profile, and its investment environment.

Key Functions of Money:

1. **Medium of exchange**
2. **Unit of account**
3. **Store of value**

When any of these functions deteriorate due to inflation, instability, or political mismanagement **confidence collapses**, and economic disruption follows.

9.2 Fiat Currency Systems vs. the Gold Standard

The Gold Standard (Classical and Bretton Woods)

- Money was backed by a fixed quantity of gold.
- Limited central bank discretion.
- Imposed fiscal and trade discipline.
- Favored long-term price stability.
- **Strengths:** Trusted store of value, constrained inflation.
  Weaknesses: Inflexibility during crises, constrained stimulus, susceptibility to deflation.

Fiat Currency System (Post-1971)

- Money is created by central banks without gold backing.
- Greater policy flexibility (QE, interest rate manipulation).
- Credit expansion is theoretically unlimited.

Strengths: Adaptability, monetary sovereignty.

Weaknesses: Prone to inflation, currency devaluation, and policy misuse.

Today, **all major currencies are fiat**, and trust in them is underpinned by **confidence in central banks and governments** not intrinsic value.

9.3 Currency Devaluation and Inflation

Currency Devaluation:

- A country's central bank or government **reduces the value** of its currency relative to others.
- Commonly used to improve **trade competitiveness** or reduce real debt burdens.

Risks:

- Imported inflation
- Capital flight
- Loss of investor confidence

Hyperinflation:

- An extreme, rapid loss of purchasing power often driven by uncontrolled money printing, collapsing institutions, or war.
- Typically leads to currency rejection, barter systems, or dollarization.

9.4 Capital Controls and Monetary Sovereignty

When currencies are under stress, governments often resort to **capital controls** restrictions on cross-border flows of money and investment.

- Limits on foreign exchange transactions
- Taxes on foreign investments
- Quotas or bans on foreign remittances

While such controls can stabilize short-term panic, they often erode **long-term investment trust**.

Monetary sovereignty a nation's ability to control its own currency and interest rates is critical, but it only works if the currency is **credible and accepted** domestically and internationally.

9.5 The Role of the IMF, World Bank, and Global Debt

International institutions like the **International Monetary Fund (IMF)** and **World Bank** act as stabilizers for the global monetary system.

IMF

- Provides emergency funding and debt restructuring support
- Imposes conditions on fiscal reform and structural adjustments
- Acts as lender of last resort for nations in crisis

World Bank

- Funds infrastructure and development projects
- Supports long-term poverty reduction and institutional capacity

These institutions help prevent **contagion and systemic collapse**, but they are often criticized for imposing **austerity policies** that harm vulnerable populations.

9.6 Case Studies: Currency Crises in Action

Latin America (1980s–2000s)

- **Argentina**, **Brazil**, **Mexico**, and **Venezuela** all faced cycles of devaluation, inflation, and IMF bailouts.
- Triggered by fiscal deficits, external debt, and political mismanagement.
- Many countries experienced **lost decades** of development.

Turkey (2018–2023)

- Massive inflation driven by unorthodox monetary policy.
- Erdogan's refusal to raise interest rates despite rising prices eroded currency credibility.
- Result: lira collapse, capital controls, dollarization of savings.

Zimbabwe (2000s–Present)

- Land seizures, fiscal collapse, and hyperinflation led to **complete currency rejection**.

- At its peak, inflation reached **89.7 sextillion percent**.
- The economy now operates primarily on U.S. dollars and South African rand.

These examples illustrate how poor monetary governance devastates currencies and how **credibility is hard to win, easy to lose.**

9.7 Digital Currencies and the Future of Money

Central Bank Digital Currencies (CBDCs)

- Government-issued digital money
- Already live in countries like China (e-CNY), Nigeria, and the Bahamas
- Offers greater control over monetary policy and surveillance

Crypto-Currencies

- Decentralized alternatives like Bitcoin, Ethereum
- Offer portability, censorship resistance, and finite supply
- Still face volatility, regulatory threats, and limited adoption

Currency Wars and Fragmentation

- Countries are developing **alternative payment systems** to SWIFT (e.g., China's CIPS).
- De-dollarization efforts aim to reduce U.S. financial hegemony.
- These shifts could lead to a **bifurcated global currency system** with multiple regional "anchors."

9.8 Investor Implications: Navigating Monetary Risk

1. Hedge Currency Risk

- Use **currency-hedged ETFs** or derivatives
- Own assets denominated in **multiple currencies**
- Avoid overexposure to a single economy

2. Own Real Assets

- Gold, commodities, real estate **retain value during currency crises**
- Inflation-linked bonds (TIPS) can protect against rising prices

3. Monitor Central Bank Behavior

- Track interest rate paths, inflation targets, and reserve adequacy
- Be cautious in countries where **policy independence is eroding**

4. Follow External Debt Ratios

- Countries with high **foreign-denominated debt** are more vulnerable to devaluation spirals

9.9 Summary: Money as a Trust-Based System

Modern currencies are no longer backed by gold but by **confidence in institutions**. When that confidence falters, so does the value of money itself.

Key takeaways:

- Understand the system you're investing in: fiat, gold, or digital
- Watch inflation, devaluation, and debt metrics
- Diversify across currencies and jurisdictions
- Favor real assets and inflation hedges when monetary risk rises

CHAPTER 10

FISCAL POLICY AND WEALTH DISTRIBUTION

10.1 Understanding Fiscal Policy: The Government's Economic Lever

While central banks influence economies through **monetary policy**, governments do so through **fiscal policy** the management of taxation and public spending.

Fiscal policy impacts:

- Aggregate demand
- Income distribution
- Investment incentives
- Debt levels and creditworthiness

In contrast to monetary tools, fiscal policy **targets the real economy more directly** stimulating growth through infrastructure, education, social programs, or defense. But it also has the potential to **distort incentives**, widen inequality, or trigger inflation if misused.

10.2 The Components of Fiscal Policy

1. Taxation

- Income tax, corporate tax, VAT/sales tax, capital gains tax
- Shapes incentives to work, save, and invest
- Progressive taxation can reduce inequality; regressive taxes can worsen it

2. Government Spending

- Entitlements: Social Security, Medicare, unemployment benefits
- Investments: infrastructure, R&D, education
- Transfers: subsidies, pensions, basic income

3. Budget Balance and Deficits

- A deficit occurs when **spending exceeds revenue**
- Funded via borrowing (issuing government bonds)
- Long-term deficits increase **public debt-to-GDP**

10.3 Inequality: The Economic and Political Consequences

The past four decades have seen rising **wealth and income inequality** in many countries—especially developed economies like the U.S.

Causes include:

- Globalization and outsourcing
- Technology displacing low-skilled jobs
- Tax policy favoring capital over labor
- Declining unionization and wage bargaining power

Consequences:

- **Lower consumer demand** (the wealthy spend a smaller share of income)
- **Political polarization** and populism
- **Health and education disparities**
- Reduced **social mobility** and trust in institutions

10.4 Populism and Political Instability

Inequality breeds **populist backlash** movements that reject the political and economic status quo in favor of more radical redistribution or nationalism.

Examples:

- **Brexit** in the UK
- **Trumpism** in the U.S.

- **Yellow Vests** in France
- Leftist-populist movements in Latin America

Populism can lead to:

- Protectionist trade policies
- Capital flight
- Erosion of institutional independence
- Unpredictable tax and regulatory changes

Investors must monitor **political risk as a key macro variable**, especially in election years.

10.5 The Fiscal Multiplier: When Does Spending Work?

Not all government spending is equal. The **fiscal multiplier** measures how much economic output increases for each $1 of government spending.

High Multipliers:

- Infrastructure projects
- Emergency transfers (e.g. stimulus checks during COVID)
- Spending in recessions

Low or Negative Multipliers:

- Debt service payments
- Defense spending in overheated economies
- Tax cuts for the wealthy in high-debt countries

Understanding where and when fiscal stimulus is effective is crucial for both policymakers and investors.

10.6 Universal Basic Income (UBI): An Emerging Debate

UBI proposes giving every citizen a **fixed, unconditional cash transfer** usually monthly.

Arguments for UBI:

- Simplifies welfare systems
- Reduces poverty
- Helps workers adjust to automation and job loss

- Stimulates demand in low-income communities

Arguments against:

- Expensive to fund at meaningful levels
- Potential to reduce labor participation
- Politically controversial
- May crowd out other social investments

Pilot Programs:

- Finland, Canada, Kenya, and U.S. cities like Stockton have tested small-scale UBI initiatives.
- Results show improved **mental health, job-seeking behavior, and financial stability**, but scaling remains a challenge.

10.7 Fiscal Dominance and the Limits of Monetary Policy

In high-debt environments, central banks may be pressured to **accommodate fiscal deficits** keeping interest rates low to ensure government debt remains serviceable.

This is known as **fiscal dominance.**

Risks include:

- Inflation if central banks lose independence
- Undermining of currency credibility
- Asset bubbles if interest rates are held too low for too long

Investors should watch for signs that fiscal priorities are overriding sound monetary management especially in election cycles or crises.

10.8 Investing in Unequal Societies

Inequality has both direct and indirect implications for markets.

Risks:

- Unpredictable regulation or taxation
- Social unrest disrupting production and supply chains
- Reputational risk for companies perceived as exploitative

Opportunities:

- Companies focused on affordable healthcare, education, and housing
- Investments in inclusive fin-tech and digital access
- Green infrastructure targeting underserved communities

ESG Integration:

Investors increasingly assess **"S" (Social) metrics** in ESG frameworks looking at pay equity, workforce]diversity, and community impact.

10.9 Summary: The Fiscal Equation for the 21st Century

As the post-globalization world becomes more fragmented, governments will play a larger role in shaping economies. Fiscal policy is no longer a background issue it's a central driver of growth, inflation, inequality, and market sentiment.

Key takeaways:

- Inequality is not just a moral concern it's a **macroeconomic and investment risk**
- Fiscal policy must strike a balance between **stimulus and sustainability**
- Populism is reshaping fiscal agendas across the globe
- Investors must analyze political trajectories, tax regimes, and government debt trends as core parts of macro strategy

CHAPTER 11

PRINCIPLES FOR ASSET ALLOCATION

11.1 The Core Challenge: Allocating Capital in a Complex World

At the heart of every investor's task lies one fundamental question:

How should I allocate my capital across different assets, markets, and environments to achieve sustainable returns and manage risk?

Asset allocation is the single most important determinant of long-term portfolio performance. Far more than picking the right stocks or timing the market, **how you spread your exposure across asset classes** equities, bonds, cash, commodities, real estate defines your success.

But in a world of:

- Economic uncertainty,
- Monetary instability,
- Geopolitical fragmentation, and
- Technological disruption,

Traditional models must evolve. This chapter lays out the **principles and tools** to build portfolios that are both **resilient and dynamic**.

11.2 Strategic vs. Tactical Allocation

Strategic Allocation:

- Long-term blueprint based on risk tolerance, goals, time horizon
- Examples: 60/40 equity/bond portfolio; risk parity framework
- Adjusted only when major changes in objectives or assumptions occur

Tactical Allocation:

- Short- to medium-term adjustments based on current economic and market conditions
- Responds to cycles, regime shifts, valuations, or geopolitical risk

Key Insight:

Strategic allocation is the foundation. Tactical allocation is the steering wheel.

11.3 Core Asset Classes and Their Roles

Each asset class has distinct characteristics and plays a unique role in a portfolio:

Asset Class	Role	Pros	Cons
Equities	Growth	Capital appreciation, dividend income	Volatile, sensitive to cycles
Bonds	Stability / Income	Predictable cash flow, lower volatility	Vulnerable to inflation and rate hikes
Cash	Liquidity / Optionality	Preserves capital, easy access	Erodes with inflation
Commodities	Inflation Hedge	Real asset exposure, low correlation	High volatility, no income
Real Estate	Income / Hard Asset	Rents, tangible value, inflation buffer	Illiquidity, cyclical risk
Alternatives	Diversification	Low correlation, alpha potential	Complexity, fees, access limits

11.4 Adjusting for Inflation, Rates, and Risk Premia

In today's volatile world, a static allocation is insufficient. Asset classes perform differently depending on macro conditions:

Inflationary Environments:

- Favor: commodities, gold, inflation-linked bonds, real assets
- Avoid: long-duration bonds, cash

Rising Interest Rates:

- Favor: short-duration bonds, value stocks, floating-rate debt
- Avoid: high-growth equities, long-term Treasuries

Disinflationary or Deflationary Regimes:

- Favor: high-quality government bonds, growth equities, USD

Adjust portfolios dynamically based on regime signals like:

- CPI trends
- Central bank rate policy
- Yield curve shifts
- Market-based inflation expectations

11.5 Dynamic Allocation and Rebalancing Rules
Why Rebalance?

- Keeps portfolio aligned with risk profile
- Enforces discipline (buy low, sell high)
- Reduces exposure to bubble formation

Common Rebalancing Strategies:

- **Calendar-based** (e.g., quarterly or annually)
- **Threshold-based** (e.g., rebalance when a position drifts 5–10%)
- **Risk-based** (e.g., adjust based on asset volatility or drawdown risk)

Advanced Methods:

- **Trend-following overlays**: increase exposure to assets in confirmed up trends
- **Volatility targeting**: reduce risk when market volatility rises

The goal is to stay invested, stay diversified, and stay disciplined.
11.6 Risk Budgeting Frameworks
Rather than allocating capital evenly, **risk budgeting** assigns exposure based on **how much risk each asset contributes** to the portfolio.
Example:

- Stocks may represent 50% of capital but 80% of risk
- Bonds may be 40% of capital but only 10% of risk

Tools:

- **Value at Risk (VaR)**
- **Conditional VaR**

- **Expected Drawdown**
- **Beta and correlation matrices**

Risk parity is one implementation of risk budgeting but the concept applies broadly: **allocate risk, not just dollars.**

11.7 Scenario-Based Allocation

Markets are shaped by **uncertain futures**. Scenario planning helps prepare for multiple outcomes:

Scenario	Allocation Response
Stagflation	Commodities, gold, inflation-protected bonds
Strong growth, low inflation	Equities, real estate, high-yield debt
Recession	Government bonds, defensive equities, cash
Crisis / liquidity shock	Short-term Treasuries, gold, put options

Run your portfolio through stress scenarios and test:

- Drawdown risk
- Liquidity risk
- Performance dispersion

11.8 Common Asset Allocation Pitfalls

- **Home bias** (overweight domestic equities)
- **Overconcentration** in equities during bull markets
- **Underestimating correlations** during crises
- **Neglecting real assets and inflation hedges**
- **Failing to update assumptions** (e.g., bonds are not always safe)

Resilient portfolios require **self-awareness, humility, and flexibility**.

11.9 Summary: Build with Intent, Adapt with Intelligence

Asset allocation is not a set-it-and-forget-it exercise. It is an **ongoing discipline**, grounded in purpose and responsive to change.

Key takeaways:

- Diversify not just by asset type, but by **economic exposure**
- Balance long-term conviction with short-term adaptation

- Allocate based on **risk**, not just capital
- Use rules to remove emotion and enhance consistency

CHAPTER 12

EMOTIONAL DISCIPLINE AND BIAS AWARENESS

12.1 Why Psychology Shapes Performance

Even the most sophisticated investment strategies can fail if not executed with emotional discipline. The data is clear:

- Most retail investors **underperform their own investments** due to emotional buying and selling.
- Professionals, too, fall victim to **confirmation bias, herding behavior,** and **short-termism.**

"In the short run, markets are voting machines; in the long run, they are weighing machines." Benjamin Graham

What this quote implies is that sentiment drives short-term price action, but fundamentals prevail over time. Yet most investors are wired to react emotionally, chasing performance or fleeing volatility usually at the wrong time.

12.2 Common Investor Fallacies and Cognitive Biases

Let's break down the most common **cognitive traps** and how they affect investment decisions:

1. Loss Aversion

- Losses feel **twice as painful** as equivalent gains.
- Leads to holding losers too long or selling winners too early.

2. Confirmation Bias

- Seeking only information that supports one's views.
- Leads to poor decision-making and missed red flags.

3. Herding

- Following the crowd during booms or busts.
- "Everyone is buying tech stocks—I should too."

4. Recency Bias

- Overweighting recent experiences.
- Assuming what happened yesterday will happen tomorrow.

5. Overconfidence

- Belief in one's forecasting ability despite data showing otherwise.
- Results in excessive trading, poor diversification, or leverage misuse.

6. Anchoring

- Fixating on a reference point (e.g., past stock price or purchase price).
- Inhibits objective reassessment.

7. Disposition Effect

- Tendency to sell winners and hold losers opposite of what logic suggests.

Recognizing these patterns is the first step to mitigating them.

12.3 Tools for Cultivating Emotional Discipline

Discipline is not a personality trait it's a system. These practices can help enforce consistency:

1. Use Predefined Rules

- Rebalancing schedules
- Stop-loss orders
- Asset allocation bands

2. Automate Where Possible

- Systematic contributions and withdrawals
- Robo-advisors or algorithmic overlays for trade execution

3. Keep an Investment Journal

- Record every investment decision and rationale
- Review periodically to identify emotional or irrational patterns

4. Implement Checklists

- Before entering a trade: "What am I assuming? What could go wrong?"
- During stress: "What are my long-term goals?"

12.4 Radical Transparency and Feedback Loops

Inspired by Bridgewater's culture, **radical transparency** encourages rigorous self-examination and feedback:

- Acknowledge mistakes openly
- Solicit critical feedback from others
- Maintain accountability through written plans

This isn't just about investing it's about developing **intellectual humility**, which is vital in a world of uncertainty.

12.5 The Power of Meditation and Reflection

Research shows that **emotional regulation tools**, like meditation or journaling, can improve investment outcomes by enhancing:

- **Cognitive clarity**
- **Impulse control**
- **Self-awareness**

Bridgewater encourages daily reflection for decision-makers, believing that "**Pain + Reflection = Progress**." This formula helps turn losses or setbacks into **learning loops** rather than trauma points.

12.6 Designing a Behavioral Risk Management System

You can't eliminate emotion but you can design your environment to **minimize its influence**.

Design Principles:

- Predefine your reactions to major market events
- Separate **research time** from **decision time**
- Limit media exposure during high-volatility periods
- Avoid over-monitoring portfolios (more screen time = more mistakes)

Build Friction:

- Use delay tactics before executing discretionary trades (e.g., 24-hour rule)
- Require justification and documentation for major allocation changes

These micro-systems create **cognitive firewalls** they protect your investment plan from your own psychology.

12.7 When to Break the Rules And How

Systems should guide behavior, not imprison it. Occasionally, **rules must be broken** but only if:

- The deviation is planned and documented
- The rationale is based on data, not fear or hype
- The new course of action aligns with long-term goals

"Principles can be bent for cause, but never broken without consequence."

This approach balances **discipline with flexibility**, a rare but vital combination in investing.

12.8 Summary: Mind Over Markets

Markets are uncertain. Your mind is noisy. The edge lies in mastering the **interface between the two**.

Key takeaways:

- Emotional discipline often matters more than strategy
- Biases are predictable and preventable with systems
- Radical transparency, reflection, and feedback can elevate your edge
- Build structures to support rational action in irrational times

With psychology in check, we now approach the final layer of portfolio design **preparing for crisis and rare events** that can wipe out gains and challenge even the best systems.

CHAPTER 13

CRISIS PREPAREDNESS AND BLACK SWAN EVENTS

13.1 The Nature of Black Swan Events

Black Swan events rare, unpredictable occurrences with severe consequences can reshape economies, markets, and entire investment paradigms.

Examples include:

- The **2008 Global Financial Crisis**
- The **COVID-19 pandemic and 2020 crash**
- The **2011 Fukushima nuclear disaster**
- The **Russia-Ukraine conflict** (2022–)
- The **9/11 terrorist attacks**

These events share three qualities:

1. **Extreme impact**
2. **Low probability (in hindsight, poorly anticipated)**
3. **High levels of systemic interconnectedness**

"What you don't see coming is what hurts the most."

13.2 Resilience vs. Fragility: A Portfolio's Core Attribute

Portfolios can be designed to be **resilient** or **fragile** under stress.

Fragile Portfolios:

- Over-concentrated in one asset class (e.g., equities)
- Highly leveraged
- Inflexible or over-optimized for specific conditions

Resilient Portfolios:

- Diversified across multiple regimes
- Include real assets, cash buffers, and hedges
- Use dynamic rebalancing and scenario testing

Resilience doesn't eliminate risk it spreads and absorbs it so that no single event destroys the whole.

13.3 Dalio's Crisis Playbook: Principles for Surviving Rare Events

Ray Dalio outlines three principles for navigating chaos:

1. Prepare for the Worst-Case Scenario

- Assume things can go much worse than consensus expects.
- Build **margin of safety** in allocations and leverage.

2. Understand That Risk Is What You Don't See

- True risk is not volatility it's **the hidden exposure you forgot to check.**
- Monitor tail risk and correlated breakdowns.

3. Stay Calm, Objective, and Data-Driven in Crises

- Panic is not a strategy.
- Use predefined action plans and decision checklists during stress.

13.4 Portfolio Techniques for Crisis Readiness

1. Tail Risk Hedging

- Protective puts on equities
- Long volatility positions (e.g., VIX derivatives)
- Long U.S. Treasuries or cash equivalents

2. Cash Buffers and Dry Powder

- Maintain liquidity to meet obligations and capitalize on dislocation.
- Don't rely solely on credit lines during market stress they may freeze.

3. Crisis Assets

- **Gold**: store of value during inflation or panic
- **U.S. Treasuries**: flight-to-safety instruments
- **Long-duration sovereign debt** (in disinflationary shocks)

4. Diversify Across Geographies and Systems

- Invest in economies that **aren't correlated** politically or economically.
- Maintain exposure to **different currencies**, not just USD or EUR.

13.5 Mental Models for Navigating Uncertainty

In a crisis, rational thought can be overwhelmed by fear. Mental models help reduce noise:

Barbell Strategy

- Split between ultra-safe assets and high-risk/high-reward assets
- Avoid "medium risk" bets that offer little protection or payoff

Antifragility

- A concept by Nassim Nicholas Taleb
- Systems that gain from disorder (e.g., adaptive strategies, volatility trading)

First Principles Thinking

- Strip situations down to fundamental truths
- Rebuild understanding without relying on flawed assumptions

13.6 Case Study: 2008 Global Financial Crisis

What Happened:

- U.S. housing bubble burst
- Lehman Brothers collapsed
- Interbank lending froze

What Worked:

- Long U.S. Treasuries
- Systematic strategies with predefined sell triggers
- Gold, briefly

What Didn't:

- Leveraged long-only equity portfolios
- Complex derivatives (CDOs, synthetic products)
- Blind trust in ratings agencies and models

Lessons:

- Liquidity evaporates faster than expected
- Correlations converge in panic
- Being early to reduce risk is better than being reactive

13.7 Case Study: COVID-19 Crash and Response

What Happened:

- Global economy shut down within weeks
- Stocks dropped 30–35% in under a month
- Central banks launched record stimulus measures

What Worked:

- Fast-acting trend-following systems
- Treasuries (early phase)
- Tech and stay-at-home stocks during recovery
- Long volatility positions

What Didn't:

- Airlines, energy, travel
- Buy-and-hold without adjustment
- Unhedged leverage

Lessons:

- Modern crises unfold **faster and with more volatility** than ever
- Policy response can reverse sentiment rapidly
- Being positioned for both outcomes matters more than being right

13.8 Checklist: Crisis Readiness for Investors

◈ Do I have cash or liquid reserves?
◈ Is my portfolio over-leveraged or concentrated?
◈ Do I have uncorrelated assets or hedges?
◈ Have I stress-tested my portfolio for extreme scenarios?
◈ Do I have written action plans for draw-downs and dislocations?
◈ Can I remain calm and rational under pressure?

This checklist should be **reviewed quarterly**, just like rebalancing.

13.9 Summary: Prepare, Don't Predict

You cannot forecast Black Swans, but you can **engineer robustness**.
Key takeaways:

- Build margin of safety through cash, hedges, and diversification
- Use systems to stay rational when emotions surge
- Protect against tail risk, then be ready to act when others panic
- Surviving the crash is more important than predicting it

CHAPTER 14

TECHNOLOGY AND THE NEW ECONOMY

14.1 Technology as the Next Great Economic Driver

Since the dawn of industrialization, technology has been the **primary catalyst** of long-term productivity growth and investment opportunity. In the 21st century, we are witnessing an exponential acceleration in technological advancement driven by:

- Artificial Intelligence (AI)
- Automation and robotics
- Quantum computing
- Decentralized finance (DeFi)
- Biotech and longevity science
- Space technologies

This shift is not evolutionary it is **transformational**, redefining entire industries, labor markets, and value chains.

14.2 The Fourth Industrial Revolution

Coined by Klaus Schwab of the World Economic Forum, the **Fourth Industrial Revolution** marks the fusion of technologies across the physical, digital, and biological realms.

Characteristics:

- Speed and scale of change
- Blurring of boundaries between industries
- Increased reliance on data and machine learning
- Cyber-physical systems: devices that sense, compute, and act in real time

"We are not just experiencing a tech boom. We are experiencing a civilizational shift in how value is created."

14.3 Disruption of Traditional Industries

Technology is not just creating new industries it's disrupting old ones. Here's how:

Finance

- Traditional banks are being disinter-mediated by fin-tech, neo-banks, and decentralized platforms.
- Payments, lending, and investing are being **automated and digitized**.

Healthcare

- Diagnostics and treatment increasingly powered by AI and wearable tech
- Precision medicine and genetic editing transforming patient outcomes
- Startups now challenge pharma giants in speed and agility

Energy

- The shift toward **decarbonization** is favoring renewables, battery storage, and smart grids
- Energy majors are being forced to **reinvent themselves or decline**

Manufacturing

- Automation and 3D printing are enabling on-demand, localized production
- Supply chains are becoming more **resilient and intelligent**

Real Estate and Retail

- The rise of remote work and e-commerce has altered **space utilization patterns**
- Digital infrastructure (data centers, cloud warehouses) is the new "prime location"

14.4 Investing in Emerging Technologies

Key Themes for the Decades Ahead:

- **Artificial Intelligence and Machine Learning**

- **Semiconductors and Advanced Materials**
- **Clean Energy and Climate Tech**
- **Biotechnology and Longevity Science**
- **Blockchain Infrastructure and DeFi**
- **Space Exploration and Satellite Networks**

How to Gain Exposure:

- **Public equities** (e.g., ETFs, thematic funds)
- **Private equity / venture capital** (higher risk, illiquidity)
- **Startups and crowd platforms**
- **Strategic indexes and AI-curated portfolios**

Investors must balance **visionary conviction with risk control**—many new tech ventures fail, but a few can transform industries.

14.5 Risks of Technological Disruption

1. Job Displacement and Social Backlash

- AI and automation may displace millions of workers
- Without proper retraining, inequality could rise

2. Data Privacy and Cybersecurity

- Increased digitalization raises vulnerability to attacks
- Regulation is lagging innovation

3. Monopolization and Platform Dominance

- A handful of tech firms control vast data and influence
- Antitrust and national security concerns are rising

4. Techno-Authoritarianism

- Surveillance tools used for state control
- Export of digital repression technologies to developing nations

Investors should consider **ethical exposure** and **regulatory headwinds** when evaluating tech plays.

14.6 The Role of Artificial Intelligence in Investing

AI is rapidly becoming a core component of asset management and market analysis.

Applications:

- Portfolio optimization
- Predictive analytics (macroeconomic forecasting, market sentiment)
- Real-time fraud detection
- Algorithmic trading
- Client personalization in wealth management

Challenge: Human oversight is still critical. AI models can **overfit**, misinterpret context, or act unpredictably under stress.

Opportunity: Blending human judgment with machine efficiency.

14.7 Strategic Framework: Tech-Informed Portfolio Design

Investors can position portfolios to benefit from technological tailwinds through:

- **Thematic allocation** (e.g., AI, robotics, clean tech ETFs)
- **Barbell strategy** (core stable assets + high-growth tech exposure)
- **Private-public hybrid portfolios** (early-stage and listed investments)
- **Innovation funds** (managed by firms with deep R&D knowledge)

Watch for: Valuation bubbles, hype cycles, and regulatory disruption.

14.8 Summary: The Future Will Be Built by Code, Capital, and Courage

Technology is not just a sector it's the **substrate of the new economy**. It will shape not only which companies win, but which nations thrive and which fall behind.

Key takeaways:

- The pace of change is accelerating investors must keep learning and adapting
- Exposure to technological innovation is essential, but must be balanced
- Societal, ethical, and regulatory dimensions are now integral to investment analysis
- The most valuable companies of tomorrow may not exist today

CHAPTER 15

SUSTAINABILITY AND ESG PRINCIPLES

15.1 The ESG Revolution in Finance

A decade ago, ESG investing was niche largely associated with impact funds, ethical screens, and socially conscious endowments. Today, it's a **mainstream force**, driving trillions of dollars in capital flows and redefining how risk and opportunity are measured.

ESG = Environmental, Social, and Governance

Factor	Key Focus
Environmental	Climate change, emissions, natural resource use, energy efficiency
Social	Labor practices, diversity & inclusion, customer impact, human rights
Governance	Board structure, transparency, executive pay, anti-corruption

"Sustainability is no longer just a moral imperative. It's an investment one."

15.2 Why ESG Matters for Investors

1. Risk Management

- Climate risk is now **financial risk**
- Social unrest and poor governance lead to underperformance, fines, and reputational damage

2. Long-Term Alpha

- Companies with strong ESG profiles tend to be **better run, more resilient**, and **more adaptable**
- ESG outperformance during COVID-19 volatility was a proof point

3. Regulatory Trends

- Europe mandates ESG disclosures (SFDR, EU Taxonomy)
- U.S. SEC is increasing enforcement and transparency standards
- Greenwashing scrutiny is rising

4. Client Demand

- Millennials and Gen Z favor investments aligned with values
- Institutions (e.g., pension funds) require ESG compliance

15.3 Environmental Sustainability: Climate and Capital

Key Themes for Investors:

- **Carbon pricing** and emissions regulation
- **Renewable energy** and clean tech
- **Climate adaptation** infrastructure (resilient agriculture, flood protection)
- **Stranded assets**: Fossil fuels and industrial real estate at long-term risk

Transition Risks vs. Physical Risks:

- **Transition**: Cost of shifting away from high-emission models
- **Physical**: Cost of inaction fires, floods, resource scarcity

Investing Responses:

- Green bonds, climate ETFs, carbon credit markets
- Engagement with companies on net-zero targets

15.4 The "S" in ESG: Social Metrics in the Spotlight

In a polarized, unequal, and digitized world, social metrics are **no longer secondary.**

What investors are tracking:

- **Diversity, equity, and inclusion (DEI)**
- **Workplace safety and conditions**
- **Labor rights in supply chains**
- **Data ethics and consumer privacy**
- **Community engagement and social license to operate**

Social risks are often underappreciated until scandal hits.

15.5 Governance: The Original ESG Pillar

Poor governance often leads to fraud, underperformance, or collapse.
Key principles:

- Independent and diverse boards
- Executive compensation tied to long-term performance
- Transparent reporting and shareholder rights
- Anti-corruption and internal audit systems

Governance quality often predicts operational health.

15.6 ESG Integration vs. ESG Screening vs. Impact Investing

Strategy	Description	Trade-offs
ESG Integration	Incorporating ESG into financial analysis	Balanced, pragmatic
Screening	Excluding or including firms based on ethical criteria (e.g., tobacco, fossil fuels)	May reduce diversification
Impact Investing	Investing to generate measurable social/ environmental benefit alongside financial returns	Often long-term, lower liquidity

Modern portfolios increasingly **blend these methods.**

15.7 Debates and Criticisms of ESG

Despite its growth, ESG is not without controversy:

1. Greenwashing

- Companies and funds exaggerate sustainability credentials
- Solutions: independent audits, stricter disclosure standards

2. Lack of Standardization

- ESG scores vary widely across rating agencies
- Metrics can be inconsistent or lagging

3. Trade-offs with Returns

- Debate exists over whether ESG sacrifices or enhances performance
- Most evidence supports **long-term outperformance** but results vary by region and methodology

4. Political Pushback

- ESG has become a politicized issue in some countries (notably the U.S.)
- States banning or mandating ESG in public funds create a fragmented landscape

15.8 Sustainable Alpha: How to Invest with Purpose and Performance Best Practices:

- Use **multi-source ESG data** (not just ratings)
- Focus on **materiality** what ESG issues are most relevant to a given sector
- Engage in **active ownership** (voting, dialogue)
- Combine ESG factors with **traditional analysis** don't treat them as separate

Sectors of Opportunity:

- Clean tech, battery materials, green infrastructure
- ESG-friendly real estate
- Human capital-focused firms (e.g., workforce well-being, remote enablement)

15.9 Summary: Aligning Capital with the Long Game

ESG is no longer about virtue signaling. It's about **resilience**, **opportunity**, and **risk-adjusted performance** in a changing world.

Key takeaways:

- ESG is now a core part of due diligence and portfolio construction
- Sustainability concerns are material and growing
- Avoid simplistic ESG metrics look deeper
- Invest not just for return, but for alignment with a world worth inheriting

CHAPTER 16

THE NEXT 100 YEARS

16.1 Investing Across Centuries: The Longest View in the Room

Few investors think in 100-year time horizons. Yet the world's most enduring institutions family offices, sovereign wealth funds, endowments do. Why?

Because history shows us that:

- Civilizations rise and fall
- Monetary systems transform
- Technology reshapes life repeatedly
- Principles, not predictions, are the keys to longevity

"The farther backward you can look, the farther forward you are likely to see." Winston Churchill

This final chapter explores what the **next century** might hold and how to **invest not just for success, but for significance.**

16.2 Predicting the Unpredictable: What We Know About the Future

We can't forecast events but we can track **macro forces** likely to shape the future:

1. Demographics

- Aging populations in developed countries
- Youth booms in Africa and South Asia
- Migration tensions and policy shifts

2. Climate Change

- Rising sea levels, extreme weather, agricultural disruptions
- Pressure for decarbonization and energy transition

3. Technological Singularities

- Potential for AI to surpass human cognitive capacity
- Biotechnology breakthroughs in lifespan and healthspan

- Quantum computing redefining encryption, modeling, logistics

4. New Economic Orders

- Multipolar geopolitics replacing U.S.-led dominance
- Rise of new reserve currencies or digital monetary blocs
- Resource wars (water, energy, food security)

5. Values and Systems Transformation

- Future of capitalism: stakeholder vs shareholder
- Redefinition of human rights in digital space
- Expansion of universal basic income, global wealth redistribution mechanisms

16.3 Lessons from Past Centuries

Looking back helps us calibrate forward:

Era	Shift
19th Century	Industrial revolution, empires, early globalization
20th Century	Wars, Bretton Woods, U.S. dollar supremacy, Cold War
21st Century (so far)	Tech dominance, climate urgency, rising multipolarity

Each century has pivoted on **technology, conflict, and ideology** the next will too.

16.4 The Future of Capitalism and Wealth

Capitalism will endure but it may evolve:

- **From extraction to regeneration**: Emphasis on circular economies, natural capital
- **From ownership to access**: Platform models, gig economies, tokenization
- **From isolated wealth to systems stewardship**: Investors held accountable for externalities

Long-term investors must navigate:

- **Higher volatility**

- **Moral complexity**
- **Multi-stakeholder expectations**

16.5 Principles for Intergenerational Wealth and Impact

1. Think in Cycles and Systems

- Understand debt cycles, power shifts, tech booms, and ecological feedback loops

2. Design for Adaptation

- Build flexible portfolios that evolve with changing regimes

3. Prioritize Resilience Over Maximization

- Survival through crises enables future growth

4. Measure Success Beyond Returns

- Impact, reputation, societal contribution, and long-term stability

5. Teach the Next Generation

- Wealth without wisdom is fleeting
- Embed principles, ethics, and history in family or institutional governance

16.6 What Legacy-Oriented Investors Must Do Now

- Diversify globally, across time horizons and regimes
- Invest in education, innovation, and sustainability
- Document investment philosophies and principles
- Fund systems not just products or companies that build the future
- Balance optimism with humility

The true investor is not a speculator but a steward of capital, vision, and civilization.

16.7 Final Thoughts: From Cycle Awareness to Strategic Legacy

This book began by breaking down the mechanics of economies and debt cycles. It moved through investment systems, geopolitics, emotional resilience, and emerging technologies. We now end with a vision:

That principled, systems-aware investors armed with historical perspective and ethical clarity can build **portfolios, organizations, and legacies** that endure not just years or decades, but across centuries.

Let the next 100 years begin.

www.ingramcontent.com/pod-product-compliance
Lightning Source LLC
LaVergne TN
LVHW022107200926
848481LV00003B/1079
9781088262177